# AMERICAN
# MUSCLE
# SUPERCARS

*Ultimate Street Performance from*
*Shelby, Baldwin-Motion, Mr. Norm*
*and Other Legendary Tuners*

## DAVID NEWHARDT

First published in 2008 by Motorbooks, an imprint of MBI Publishing Company, 400 First Avenue North, Suite 300, Minneapolis, MN 55401 USA

Motorbooks titles are also available at discounts in bulk quantity for industrial or sales-promotional use. For details write to Special Sales Manager at MBI Publishing Company, 400 First Avenue North, Suite 300, Minneapolis, MN 55401 USA.

To find out more about our books, join us online at www.motorbooks.com.

Library of Congress Cataloging-in-Publication Data

Newhardt, David, 1955–
  American muscle supercars / David Newhardt.
     p. cm.
  Includes index.
  ISBN 978-0-7603-3294-8 (hb w/ jkt)
  1.  Muscle cars—United States—History. 2.  Sports cars—Performance—United States—History.  I. Title.

  TL23.N483 2008
  629.222—dc22

                                    2008022996

**On the cover, main:** 1969 Yenko 427 Nova.
**Inset image:** Yenko Hood.

**On the frontispiece:** 1971 Grand Spaulding Hemi Roadrunner.

**On the title pages:** 2006 Saleen S7 Twin Turbo.

**On contents page:** 1973 Baldwin-Motion Camaro.

**On the back cover, main:** 1969 Royal Bobcat GTO.
**Inset image:** 2001 Berger Camaro SS.

Editor: Chris Endres
Designer: Jennifer Tischler
Jacket Design: Simon Larkin

Printed in China

# CONTENTS

# ACKNOWLEDGMENTS

Writing this book was like a treasure hunt. I never knew what information or photo I would stumble across as I dug into the histories of these dealerships. I had plenty of *"Aha!"* moments, times when the dots would connect and the fog would clear. Helping me put the pieces of the puzzle together were plenty of people that selflessly gave access to their time, their stories, and their archives. Vehicle owners opened their garages to my prying camera, and experts reviewed my text. It's said that no man is an island, and authors know this better than most. To everyone, a heartfelt *Thank You!*

In no particular order, these are the people and companies that helped in myriad ways. Dale Berger Jr., Matt Berger, Jim Luikens, Stefano Bimbi, Amy Boylan, Gary Patterson, Brian Henderson, Mel Bogus, Bob McClurg, Peyton Cramer, Dick Guldstrand, Bob Tasca Sr., Dan McMichael, Leonard and Patricia Cradit, Drew Hardin, Norm Kraus, Larry Weiner, Joel Rosen, Marty Schorr, Herb Fox, Ann Hartweg, Helen Gibb, Valerie Harrell, John Clinard, Steven Juliano, Jim Wangers, Bill & Rita Shultz, Charley Lillard, Mike Guarise, Mark Gillespie, Lynn Shelton-Zoiopoulos, David Warren, Bill Poltizer, Winston Brown, Eric Schiffer, Warren Dernoshek, Gary Dyer, Richard and Elaine Bonnefoi, Edsel Ford, Randy Leffingwell, Don McCain, Dana Mecum, Mike Mueller, Geoff Stunkard, Jim Kennedy, Keith Seymore, John Leahy, Jim Gannes, and Greg Ryden.

Special thanks go to my wife, Susan Foxx-Newhardt, and to Nora and Stella for supporting me regardless of how long I'm on the road shooting or squirreled away in my office at the computer. A tip of the hat goes to my editor, Chris Endres, who kept his cool when deadlines were flying past. Zack Miller, the Big Boss, thanks for letting me "work" in this wonderful field.

—David Newhardt
Pasadena, California 2008

# INTRODUCTION

As the American public started flipping calendar pages in the early 1960s, the automotive landscape was undergoing a radical change. Those on the leading edge of the Baby Boomer Generation were starting to make their disposable income felt in the market place. Their interests were many and varied, yet near the top of their list was having a fast car. Detroit responded by creating brutally fast automobiles, plus an extensive parts system that allowed owners to extract even more performance from their cars.

Auto dealerships across the country responded to this growing trend in a variety of ways, with a wide range of success. Many dealers entered cars in various types of competition, following the mantra "Win on Sunday, Sell on Monday." But like so many things in life, it wasn't that easy.

Running a competition car on a track to get the dealer's name in front of the public had the potential to bring in buyers, but only if a dealer played his cards right. Parking a race car on a showroom floor was interesting but rarely resulted in sales. The dealers who successfully emphasized performance had to approach the market from a number of fronts, including but not limited to service, parts, marketing, and the vehicles themselves. These dealerships never lost sight that priority number one was the selling of cars. Everything else had to play a supporting role.

It's been said that if something is easy, everyone would be doing it. Selling performance cars was a specialized skill, and the dealers who did it well could make it look easy. But a peek behind the curtain revealed an incredible amount of hard work, ambition, vision, and luck. There was no single formula for success in selling hot cars. But one constant thread ran through all the dealerships: love of performance. Without the efforts of the eleven dealerships and tuners profiled in this book, the muscle car landscape would have looked far different.

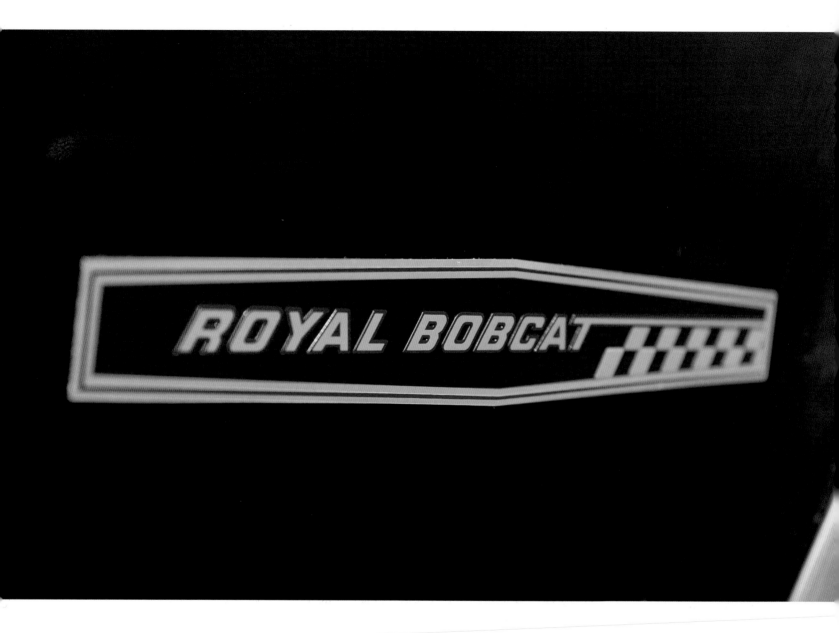

8

# CHAPTER 1

# ROYAL PONTIAC

## *IT STARTED AS AN EXPERIMENT*

It was 1959, and Dwight Eisenhower was nearing the end of his presidency as Fidel Castro started his first year as premier of Cuba. Hawaii became America's 50th state, and *Bonanza* aired on television for the first time. NASCAR was racing actual stock cars, and the NHRA was growing as thousands of drag-racing enthusiasts drove to newly minted drag strips across the country to flex their cars' muscle. At the heart of the American automobile industry, General Motors was flexing its own muscle at racing venues in an effort to grab headlines on Sunday, and buyers on Monday.

Discreet badging was a hallmark of Royal Pontiac products. Most buyers felt that the cars' performance spoke volumes. Many thought that if they had wanted performance by graphics, they would have purchased a car somewhere else.

The very embodiment of Wide-Track, the Grand Prix for 1962 cut a handsome figure. Buyers of a GP from Royal Pontiac could choose to have their new cars Bobcatted, and part of the package was a striking two-tone paint scheme.

Within the labyrinth of GM was a division in ascent, Pontiac. While the spotlight was on the traditional cross-town rivalry between Ford and Chevrolet, Pontiac was being led by Division General Manager Semon E. "Bunkie" Knudsen, a performance enthusiast who wanted the division to shed its stodgy, Mom & Pop image.

When Knudsen took over Pontiac in 1956, he immediately tasked the division with creating products with verve in an effort to shake the image problem. The 1957 Bonneville, a fuel-injected convertible that sold for the staggering sum of $5,700, was a bold first step. He brought a sharp engineer from Oldsmobile onto his team, Elliot M. "Pete" Estes. Then he hired another engineer who was looking for work following the

implosion of the Studebaker-Packard firm, John Zachary DeLorean. This trio would have an unmistakable effect on the future of Pontiac.

For the 1959 model year, a new breed of Pontiacs was going to be unleashed, incorporating a new design and a clever ad campaign, centered on the new term "Wide-Track." This phrase was more than just ad-speak; it described the result of moving the wheels as far out toward the corners of the car as possible. Knudsen had seen a styling buck in the design studio and insisted that something be done to improve the look of the full-size Pontiacs. He said that the wheels disappeared under the car. Once the changes had been made, Pontiac's advertising firm was tasked with developing a marketing campaign. One of the creative directors, Milt Coulson, thought of "Wide-Track

Pontiac's 421-cubic-inch engine earned the checkered flag many times on race tracks from coast to coast. Aluminum wheels were stylish but pricey.

Ride." A few political battles later, the Wide-Track ad blitz was in wide circulation. Done to improve the look of the full-size Pontiacs, it became the catch phrase for the Division.

One of the individuals charged with making the Wide-Track campaign work was Jim Wangers, a young assistant account executive at Pontiac's advertising agency, MacManus, John & Adams. Wangers was a car guy to the core, and had spent time working at Chevrolet and Chrysler to help shape their perform-ance images. Now he was working on the Pontiac

account and would turn out to be the right man for the job. Wangers knew the difference between racing and performance and would translate racing success into street performance success.

Knudsen had decreed that a full-court press in the racing world was the best way to get Pontiac's name in front of the public, and in that direction the Super Duty Group was created to get factory-developed high-performance parts into the right hands, both in NASCAR and NHRA. Enthusiasts could walk into a Pontiac dealership and order the same parts for their cars that the racers were using to good effect in compe-tition. The problem was Pontiac dealers didn't know where to acquire information about factory-developed and factory-distributed performance equipment.

Wangers saw that this was an opportunity to con-nect with the leading edge of the Baby Boomer Generation. If Baby Boomers could get excited about Pontiac in their late teens and early 20s, they would carry that excitement with them for life. When the old

Most drivers who challenged a Bobcatted Grand Prix tended to get familiar with this view of the vehicle. Note the Royal Bobcat emblem inboard of the passenger-side taillight. The trunk was big enough to live in.

The use of a trio of carburetors allowed the big 421-cubic-inch engine to breathe properly. Using a progressive linkage, the engine used just the center carb for most driving, but when the accelerator was floored, the front and rear carburetors kicked in, with the resulting kick in the rear.

school at GM questioned Knudsen about the traditional Pontiac buyer, he pointed out that it was far easier to sell an old man a young man's car than to sell a young man an old man's car.

Wangers presented a proposal to Knudsen and Pontiac sales manager Frank Bridges that would connect dealers with the factory at seminars at the zone offices. These seminars would give interested dealers a chance to learn about and sell performance vehicles, service, and parts. While Knudsen loved the idea, Bridges was less than enthralled.

Knudsen called Wangers later in the day, and as Wangers relates in his book *Glory Days*, said to the marketing executive, "I'll tell you what you do. Go out and find a dealer who would like to become a performance

specialist, like a guinea pig. I can't guarantee him any money, but you can tell him that the factory is interested. Tell him that if there's ever an opportunity for us to do him a favor, he can count on it."

With those marching orders, Wangers headed to the largest dealer in the area, Packer Pontiac. With three "houses," including one each in Miami, Florida, and Flint, Michigan, they seemed the ideal starting points. Wangers approached Bill Packer Jr. and laid out the concept. Packer said that it was intriguing, but he was about to head down to Florida for a month's vacation. "Let's talk when I return," he said.

Never one without a backup plan, Wangers headed immediately over to Royal Pontiac, in the Detroit suburb of Royal Oak, close to the Pontiac factory. There he

With its column-mounted tachometer and four-speed manual transmission, a Grand Prix that had enjoyed a Bobcatting session was not your normal GP. It was a heavy car, but the GP responded well to cubic inches and a heavy foot.

Placing the Royal Bobcat emblem within the side spear was a clever design feature. With the contrasting gold paint, the emblem didn't get lost in the black finish.

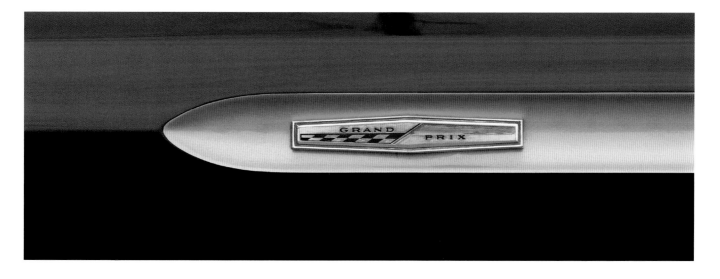

Pontiac essentially used Royal Pontiac as a front for developing race components and packages. Virtually all model Pontiacs were set up for drag racing, an arena that Pontiac excelled in during the early 1960s. During those years, drag strips were cropping up everywhere, as the NHRA was making serious efforts to get racing off of the streets and onto safe, sanctioned venues.

spoke to Asa "Ace" Wilson Jr. The son of the part-owner of a successful dairy business, Ira Wilson Dairy, he wasn't the least bit interested in milk and cheese. He was a lover of wine, women, and cars. When his father, Asa Sr., saw that Ace Jr. lacked the self-starting gene, he bought a small Pontiac dealership in Royal Oak and installed his son there to run it.

When first opened, it was simply called Royal Pontiac. It was a modest success, and after a while, as sales increased, the name grew to be Ace Wilson's Royal Pontiac. Then in September 1959, Jim Wangers walked into the showroom with a proposal. As Ace Jr. listened, he grew excited. He genuinely loved cars and was open enough to try something new. That day, he committed Royal Pontiac to this experiment.

The first step was to stock the right Super Duty "speed" parts. Next came a bigger hurdle—teaching the sales staff that money could be made in pushing performance. Most of the salesmen scoffed at the idea of people actually coming in and ordering a performance car. However, Royal was fortunate to have a performance enthusiast among its showroom sales staff, Dick Jesse. Wangers saw that Jesse "got" the performance thrust that Wangers and Pontiac were trying at Royal and soaked up all of the information he could about muscle Pontiacs. This effort soon paid dividends for Jesse, as customers hungry for performance-optioned cars would be directed to him.

The rest of the sales staff couldn't and wouldn't understand the fascination with high horsepower. Their

The most important part of a Pontiac GTO was the powerplant, and when the mechanics at Royal Pontiac turned their attention to the blue V-8, the result was a nice increase in power and crisper throttle response.

interest lay in selling "regular" vehicles. Yet when customers would patiently wait in line to talk with Jesse, and his paycheck would fatten, they felt more than a bit jealous. Some of them tried to emulate Jesse, but their hearts weren't in it, and the customers could pick that up in an instant. They went with a salesman who spoke their language.

Jesse immediately assumed the role of "Performance Sales Manager," and the word quickly got out on the street that if you wanted a fast Pontiac, this was the guy to see. Jesse would work hard to make sure the customer ended up with a car that fit his or her needs. If there was a question as to whether some equipment was worth it, Jesse would give the customer a ride in a fast demo, often heading north of the dealership to a straight stretch of road through a cemetery. As there was nowhere for the police to hide, it was a relatively safe place to briefly flex the Pontiac's muscle. This ride would seal many a deal.

Being a marketing expert, Wangers quickly got the Royal name in front of the enthusiast market. Under the team name "Ace Wilson's Royal Pontiac," a red 1959

Catalina Hardtop Coupe was pressed into drag-strip duty. Equipped with a 389-cubic-inch, 345-horsepower V-8, Tri-Power induction system, aftermarket Isky E-2 cam, and column-shift manual three-speed transmission, it was a modest start. But it was a start.

When the 1960 models rolled out, Royal campaigned three dealership-owned cars, plus one sponsored car. Jim Wangers drove one of the two Catalinas, a red one, while Winston "Win" Brown handled driving duties in the white one. This was also the debut of a line of Pontiac-engineered parts known as Super Duty, which were intended for off-road usage only, meaning racing. The parts had been introduced at the Daytona 500 race, and within a handful of months, the parts had started trickling down to drag racers. Like all Super Duty–equipped vehicles, the Seaton Catalina had a 389-cubic-inch engine, but now it had a floor-shift four-speed manual transmission. In a nod to practicality, the car was ordered with a heater, but the insulation package was deleted. It was a non–Super Duty, 348-horsepower, 389-cubic-inch, A-engine Catalina. Equipped with an

Originally built on the Tempest platform, the 1965 GTO was the first model of GTO that was a stand alone. When Royal Pontiac would Bobcat a GTO, external indication of the modifications were virtually nil. The proof was immediately evident when the accelerator was buried.

In a shocking display of restraint, Royal Pontiac fitted these tasteful badges to the C-pillars of Royal Bobcat GTOs. During a nocturnal street race, it would be easy to miss these badges. Sneaky owners might even be tempted to leave the badges off, in an attempt to lure in more prey.

Most drivers who challenged a Royal Bobcat GTO ended up seeing this view of the street stormer. From this angle, there is nothing to indicate that the car was worked on by Ace Wilson's wrenches.

Long, graceful, and capable, the 1967 big-block GTO, as massaged by the crew at Royal Pontiac, was a straight-line beast. Like most muscle cars of the era, it could go like stink in a straight line, but unlike many of its contemporaries, it could also turn and stop without embarrassing itself.

There's nothing like the torque of a 428-cubic-inch V-8 to power everything in sight, including the air conditioning and power steering. The foam edging around the perimeter of the Ram Air box fit snugly against the bottom of the hood to prevent outside air from seeping away from the carburetors.

automatic transmission and Jim Wangers at the wheel, it won the NHRA Top Stock Eliminator class at the 1960 Nationals with a run of 14.15 seconds at 100.44 mph. At the Nationals, Royal sponsored a blue 1960 Catalina owned by a General Motors VP's son, Pete Seaton, and driven by Jack Kay. He was Wangers' competition at the big race. Royal got a load of publicity, and the dealership saw a surge in performance car sales. Ironically, at the end of the season, the red Catalina was parked on the used car lot, where it sat for three months before finally selling. Nothing's cheaper than an old race car.

Royal Pontiac offered another service that went hand in glove with the sale of performance cars, and that was a performance tuneup. A number of modifications were made, including changing the camshaft timing, ignition, spark plug gap, carburetor jetting and mechanical linkage, and thermostat. Owners were asked how they were going to use the car, as a commuter or a weekend drag racer, and then recommendations were made to maximize the car's performance while meeting the owner's budget and expectations. The result was great word of mouth, as Royal Pontiacs were cleaning up at stoplight drag races across the Midwest.

In 1961, Royal Pontiac took its involvement with street performance to a new level when it built its first Bobcat, a white Catalina Hardtop Coupe with a 389-cubic-inch Tri-Power V-8 rated at 348 horsepower. The Bobcat name was a contraction of the names Bonneville and Catalina; it denoted a vehicle that

General Motors' A-body design was a masterpiece of proportions, giving the engineers plenty of room for a large engine, a spacious interior for four adults, and a voluminous trunk, ideal for a family vacation.

enjoyed a Royal performance tuneup. Royal Bobcats were outfitted with a selection of handpicked options, including a heavy-duty suspension, a performance rear axle ratio, a tachometer, eight-lug aluminum wheels painted body color, and a Royal Bobcat tuneup treatment. Developed by Frank Rediker, the tuneup is what put the fire under the hood, and it included a progressive Tri-Power carburetor linkage, Super Duty .027-inch head gaskets to raise the compression ratio, gaskets that blocked the intake heat riser, rocker arm locker nuts, a set of special carburetor jets, and a unique distributor advance curve kit. Charlie Brumfield was now the major mechanic installing Bobcat treatments until 1965, when the GTO started filling the service bays.

Royal went to the 1961 NHRA Nationals at Indianapolis looking to repeat the victory from the prior year. Two Super Duty vehicles were set up and taken to the strip, one with an automatic transmission and one with a manual. The team, run that year by "team manager" Ace Wilson Jr., didn't feel that the automatic-equipped car was running as well as it should. One of the mechanics took the automatic-equipped car and did some stress-relieving donuts in a neighboring field. That didn't go over well, and the team was shown the door.

From 1961 through 1963, the name Bobcat stretched across the rear panel between the taillights in block letters sourced from the parts department bins. Starting in 1962, a handsome Royal Bobcat emblem was created, using the Grand Prix emblem as its basis. Some crafty owners would get a Royal Bobcat treatment but ask that the emblems be left off, creating a street-stomping sleeper. A number of Bonnevilles were Bobcatted as well, including the personal 1961 Bonneville convertible of Ace Wilson Jr. Wilson was

The Hurst Dual-Gate shifter was state-of-the-art for automatic transmission gear selection in 1967, while the 8-track stereo system was cutting-edge for mobile music.

close with a Teamster Union official that helped arrange delivery of four black Bonnevilles to the local's leaders, including one for Jimmy Hoffa. Of the four Bonnevilles, only Hoffa's received a Bobcat treatment.

Starting in 1962, Royal Pontiac sponsored an annual open house event, displaying its race cars as well as street Bobcats. Racing sponsors were invited to set up displays, and in the course of two days, more than 15,000 people attended the free extravaganza. A program was printed and handed out, explaining the history of Royal Pontiac's involvement in high performance and how customers could improve their Pontiacs by employing the services of Royal Pontiac's crack mechanics. The open house was held again in 1963, then again in 1968.

Ace Wilson Jr., something of a playboy, now drove a 1962 Grand Prix. But his was no ordinary Grand Prix; Jim Wangers had Frank Rediker and Win Brown install

a Paxton supercharger on it. Frank Rediker had a McCullough Blowers franchise, and as Paxton was part of his McCullough line, the technology was on the shelf. Wangers called it the "Gentleman's Hot Rod," and Brown remembers getting into trouble with it on the streets surrounding Royal Pontiac as he would "shake down" the latest improvements.

One of the most important reasons that Royal Pontiac enjoyed such success in the high-performance field was its well-stocked parts department. Run by Sam Frontera, it handled a wide array of hop-up parts, such as headers, clutches, spark plugs, springs, and anything to help both walkup and mail-order customers get that performance edge. Sam's wife, Louise, was the business manager at Royal, and she saw how the emphasis on performance was improving the bottom line. She made sure that Ace Jr. was aware of it as well.

Developed for Jim Wangers to terrify and humiliate local Detroit-area enthusiasts, this 1968 Firebird Blackbird incorporated many performance tricks learned at Royal Pontiac. Originally equipped with a Ram Air I engine and a column-shift automatic transmission, it's currently packing a brutal 455-cubic-inch engine and a massaged Turbo 400 tranny.

Pontiac introduced its 421-cubic-inch V-8 for the 1962 model year, and with Super Duty parts, it was a stormer. Before 1962, customers wanting Super Duty parts had to buy them over the counter and install them. Needless to say, Royal's 421 Super Duty was a strong presence on the dragstrip. Its best showing was 12.38 seconds at 116.23 mph. Royal mechanic Frank Rediker wrenched the big engine to generate 405 horsepower, and with the trick Pontiac-supplied parts such as an aluminum hood, inner and outer front fenders, bumper radiator panel, and trick exhaust manifolds, the vehicle weight was brought from 2 tons to around 3,600 pounds.

This was a huge improvement in a drag car, where losing a handful of pounds was considered a big deal.

On the street, Royal Pontiac was fitting street cars with performance packages, and not just Catalinas. The Grand Prix enjoyed the attention of the crack mechanics; a Paxton centrifugal supercharger blew 5.5–6 pounds of boost into the 389-cubic-inch V-8. Where a stock 389 in the GP was rated at 303 horsepower, the Royal modifications coaxed 400 ponies from the iron block.

At the end of 1962, Royal felt that the time had come to push the Royal Pontiac name nationally. The Royal Racing Team was created, a mail-order parts service, costing

The Blackbird was fitted with a Royal Automotive–built 455-cubic-inch engine, but when that engine broke, Leader Automotive constructed a new 455 engine. This powerplant will haul the Blackbird down the quarter-mile in the 10-second range.

applicants a lofty $3 for a parts catalog, membership card, window decal, and a discount on mail-order parts.

Things looked a bit rocky across the entire General Motors lineup in late 1962, as the corporation stated that it was getting out of racing—not just the commonly known arenas such as NASCAR and NHRA, but "back door" support as well. Super Duty engines became a thing of the past. Wilson felt that with Pontiac getting out of racing, maybe Royal Pontiac should too.

Fortunately there were rumors of an exciting new car on the horizon. Based on the new "A" body platform, it would end up with a 389-cubic-inch V-8, a four-speed manual transmission, and a name "borrowed" from the FIA, the GTO. Its influence would be stunning. And Royal Pontiac would ride the wave better than anyone else.

## GTO—THE GREAT ONE

Most car companies hold "long-lead" press events the summer before the new model year is debuted. This gives magazines enough time to prepare their stories

While the Blackbird wasn't built at Royal Pontiac, then-owner Jim Wangers wanted a standout paint scheme. The black/gold combo had been used at Royal Pontiac to good effect with the full line of Bobcatted cars, and with Wangers' ties to Royal, he wanted to acknowledge that connection.

The two-tone paint scheme was a Royal Pontiac exclusive, yet the buying public didn't embrace it. Perhaps this was because the typical Royal Bobcat driver preferred to remain under the radar. This flamboyant finish was anything but subtle.

The Ram Air option in Pontiac's hot cars was targeted at the drag racer. In day-to-day driving, the benefit of having a fresh-air induction system was barely felt, but on the quarter-mile, it could have a demonstrable effect.

for release at the same time the new cars are rolling into showrooms. Unfortunately for Pontiac, the late introduction of the Tempest GTO meant it was missing from the 1964 Pontiac long-lead.

When the editors of *Hot Rod* magazine requested a GTO to test in mid-1963, they were told that there weren't any in the West Coast press fleet. Eventually, the Pontiac Zone Manager, looking out for Pontiac's best interests, loaned the magazine his wife's GTO, which had been optioned as a comfortable, low-drama car. Thus it was no surprise when *Hot Rod* gave the vehicle a lukewarm review. A pissed-off Jim Wangers, confronting John DeLorean, used the article to get a pair of GTO press cars built, equipped with the "right" options. Wangers filled out the order forms and had the finished cars sent to Royal Pontiac. These cars were Bobcat-prepped and cared for by Royal Pontiac, and when journalists would visit Detroit, they were put behind

The hood-mounted tachometer was more of a marketing ploy than a legitimate performance tool. While the idea of a near eye-level tach is a good one, the distance of the instrument face from the driver and the fragility of the unit compromised its accuracy. But it sure looked cool.

Carried over from the original Royal Bobcat days, the tasteful emblem was affixed to the doors and highlighted by an accent stripe, so there was little chance of it being overlooked.

the wheel and told exactly what had been done to the car. Cue the good press. Wangers almost always told the press just what Royal Pontiac had done to each GTO so that they were aware that the Bobcat treatment made the Pontiac that much faster than stock.

Wangers brought two "special" GTOs to Florida in late December 1963 to be tested for the (in)famous March 1964 *Car and Driver* magazine article. One vehicle, painted Nocturne Blue, was fitted with a 389-cubic-inch V-8. The second GTO, finished in Buccaneer Red, had its 389 engine replaced with a healthy HO 421-cubic-inch powerplant from a Bonneville. Next stop for the red car was Royal Pontiac, where the big V-8 was given the Bobcat treatment. By grinding down a couple of distinguishing casting marks, the bigger engine was visually identical to the 389.

The magazine drove the blue GTO to their offices in New York, then down to Florida, while Wangers motored the red Pontiac south to Daytona, where *Car and Driver* ran handling tests with the blue GTO and acceleration tests on the red car. They were flabbergasted with the performance of the red car, their handheld stopwatches giving a 0–60 time of only 4.6 seconds and just 11.8 seconds for a 0–100 mph burst. Wangers kept his mouth shut and let the magazine come to its own conclusions about the GTO. The crew at Royal thought it was a hoot. Shortly

after the magazine tests, the Nocturne Blue car was crushed, as it was a pilot car and devoid of a Vehicle Identification Number. The Buccaneer Red GTO survives to this day. It wasn't until 30 years later that Wangers confessed to the engine swap.

By this time, Royal Pontiac was the unofficial front for factory Pontiac performance, where a fleet of press

Hurst had a long relationship with Pontiac, starting with the 1961 Super Duty Catalina. George Hurst was a master at promotion, and combined with the talent at Royal Pontiac, it was inevitable that memorable cars would result.

Standing by at the drag strip, this car is the source of no small amount of controversy regarding what was actually beneath the hood during the magazine test session. Regardless of which Ram Air engine was used, it was a brutally fast machine. *Shultz archives*

cars could be set up and maintained. At Wangers' insistence, Pontiac press cars were brought up to factory specs and just used for performance and media relations. When other General Motors divisions would supply a magazine writer with a car, it often came out of the zone office and was in fact an employee's driver. When that car would be matched up against a "Bobcatted" Pontiac, the results were foregone; another Pontiac triumph.

A young mechanic, Milt Schornack, arrived at Royal in October 1963 and immediately gained a reputation as a quick study. For the next 5 1/2 years, Schornack would wrench and drive Royal Pontiac's GTOs with great success on the drag strip.

Royal Pontiac clandestinely Bobcatted a 1965 Pontiac 2+2 in preparation for a *Car and Driver* article comparing it to a Ferrari 2+2. Well, at first glance, it would look like the Ferrari would embarrass the

Pontiac, but the Royal treatment helped to pull off a coup. On the drag strip, the huge Pontiac 2+2, which weighed 1,000 pounds more than the svelte Italian, beat the pure sports car. On the road track, driver Walt Hansgen flailed the Pontiac 2+2 unmercifully, coming within a half second of the Ferrari's time. During the acceleration runs, the Pontiac 2+2 was fitted with drag slicks; the magazine didn't have any problem with the Pontiac wearing them. The Royal Bobcat treatment paid off, as the big car pulled off the mind-blowing 0–60 mph time of just 3.9 seconds.

The next trick up Royal's sleeve was to tour drag strips in 1965 with a pair of GTOs, known as the GeeTO Tigers, one in white and the other painted Iris Mist with a black vinyl top. Wangers was never at a loss for promotional ideas, and the format was straightforward. Two GTOs would match race, one

Massive weight transfer lifted the heavy front end far off the ground as the rear tires were abused. Muscle cars such as this were a tire-maker's dream, as a heavy foot could waste a set of rears in a matter of minutes. *Shultz archives*

with a "Mystery Tiger" driver behind the wheel, the other car in the hands of a guest. The skilled driver, in the tiger suit, would put on a humorous show, then slide into one of the GTOs and do battle. With 10 guests going up against the Mystery Tiger, there was plenty of action to entertain the crowd. The two cars were mechanically identical, as Royal Pontiac didn't want anyone to even suggest that the contest was rigged. The Mystery Tiger would "let" the guest cross the finish line first occasionally, but he would win the majority of the day's races. It was a great way to get the GTO, and Royal Pontiac's name, in front of an appreciative audience.

This show hit the drag strip circuit again in 1966, this time running a pair of gold GTOs, one with white trim, the other with black. Two brothers, Dave and Sid Warren, joined Milt Schornack and John Polizter

handling the maintenance for the cars in 1966, and Dave Warren would fill in for John Polizter as the Mystery Tiger when needed. For 1967, the plan was again for the GTOs to be replaced with a pair of 400 Firebirds, but when the insurance company (finally) heard what the GeeTO Tiger program was all about, they blew a gasket and shut the program down, so the Mystery Tiger hung up his suit.

At the end of each racing season, Royal would roll the race cars into the service bay and prep them for sale on the lot. When the vehicle was being readied for use on the drag strip, the entire driveline would be pulled out and replaced with a race-ready setup. The original drivetrain was tucked away in a corner until the vehicle was finished with its racing duties, then out would come the racing driveline and back in went the original. If there were graphics on the car, they would be pulled off and the

This is not the first Judge to visit this location. Jim Wangers had many lunches here at the Fox & Hounds Inn on Woodward Avenue when journalists would come to Detroit to test the latest and greatest from Pontiac. This historic restaurant was located just down the road from Wangers' office.

vehicle repainted. Then it was sent out with a for-sale sign on it. Because of this practice, locating a genuine Royal race car today is like finding a needle in a haystack.

GTOs weren't the only Pontiacs that garnered attention from the hot shots at Royal. The new Firebird hit the streets late in the 1967 model year, and it wasn't long before Jim Wangers had the mechanics at Royal prepping a pair of Firebirds to use in the press fleet. The mechanics were kept busy maintaining a veritable fleet of press cars in order to keep Pontiac's, and Royal's, name front and center in the popular press.

At Royal Pontiac, the mechanics were also busy swapping out engines for customers. Pontiac had a surplus of 428 HO engines, and Royal would just go up the road to the factory and bring a big-block back

to the dealership as needed. For $650, Royal would trade out the stock 400 engine and replace it with a Bobcatted 428. These proved popular with both the public and the press.

Shortly before the Royal Racing Team was to go to the 1969 Winternationals at Pomona, California, word came down that Ace Wilson Jr. had sold the performance operation to Leader Automotive, which was owned by John DeLorean's brother, George DeLorean. John DeLorean was promoted to run Chevrolet, and without his backing and protection from corporate meddlers, the performance days at Royal were numbered. By May 1969, the dealership was no longer in the hands of Ace Wilson Jr. or Sr. George DeLorean was a successful drag racer, but he wasn't the best businessman. The mail-order parts department was

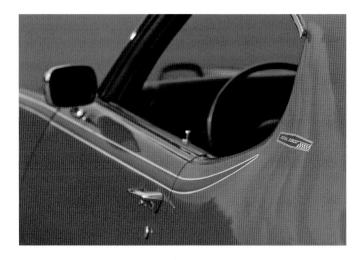

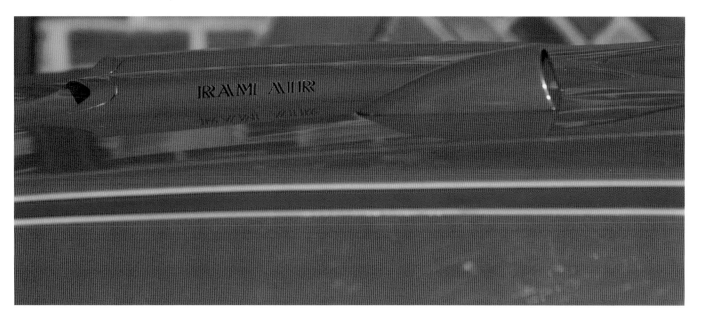

**Left:** With the splashy graphics of the Judge, Royal Pontiac didn't feel that they needed to glam up the street bruiser with additional stripes. Adding a small Royal Bobcat emblem at the base of the C-pillar was a discrete notice that this wasn't a car to trifle with.

**Below:** Small but significant, the Ram Air graphic on the hood of a Judge denoted more that just a pair of hood scoops. The engine received considerable upgrades, as Pontiac knew that many of these would see duty on the drag strip. The hood-mounted tachometer was another "performance" touch, more for show than go, but the public loved it.

neglected, with predictable results. Dick Jesse, now the performance manager at Royal Pontiac, was a crack drag racer in his own right. In 1966 Jesse raced an altered 421-cubic-inch V-8 powered GTO "funny car" under the name "Mr. Unswitchable" for his determination to stick with Pontiac when so many teams were running other brands.

In 1970, Royal Pontiac was sold to a Denver Chevrolet dealer and was renamed Bob Shaffo Pontiac. Due to customer complaints that they were being strong-armed in the showroom, Pontiac requested that the dealership be sold. Jim Fresard bought the dealership and has operated it to current times. In 2008, Fresard Pontiac-Buick-GMC left for a new facility closer to Detroit on Woodward Avenue, and the former Royal Pontiac site's future is unknown.

Ace Wilson Jr. died on March 18, 1984, yet he left behind an impressive legacy in the performance world. His dealership was the first true "performance dealer," selling "street cars" and not "race cars." Ace Wilson Jr. understood the difference between performance and racing, and with the help of a dedicated team, made money selling speed. While many others would try to emulate the operation, there was only one Royal Pontiac.

# CHAPTER 2

# NICKEY CHEVROLET

## *WINDY CITY PERFORMANCE*

There were quite a few dealerships that bet on the snappy slogan "Win on Sunday, Sell on Monday," sure that money spent at the race track would translate into money being spent in the showroom. "Hey, let's park a race car on the dealership floor and watch the customers roll in!" Too often, the reality fell short of expectations. Yet a Chicago, Illinois, Chevrolet dealership raced heavily, and the buyers flocked in. How it happened is a lesson showing how a sword cuts both ways.

Back in the day, nothing was cheaper than a couple-year-old muscle car. Bought new cheaply by kids barely out of their teens, regularly abused, then exposed to Midwestern winters, it's a wonder any Nickey muscle cars have survived. *Geoff Stunkard*

The narrow front tires were meant to keep the nose pointed in the right direction, preferably in a straight line. With a small front tire contact patch and a heavy iron big-block in front of the cowl, handling prowess was sort of low on the priority list. But if getting from A to B in the least amount of time possible was important, few cars could touch a 427 Nickey Camaro.

The story begins during the Great Depression, when Chicago, along with the rest of America, was struggling. A local dealership, located on the northwest side of the city and owned by Mr. Nickey, was purchased during the 1930s by two brothers, Edward "E. J." Stephani, and his younger sibling, John "Jack." After serving in the military during World War II, they returned to run the operation. The brothers divided the workload, with Jack running the showroom and presenting the "face" of Nickey Chevrolet, while Ed ran the back of the store, such as purchasing, finance and insurance, payroll, and the scores of behind-the-scenes transactions that keep a dealership running.

In 1957, while on vacation in Florida, Jack noticed a local business that had inserted a backward letter in its name. He remembered it as attention-getting, and when he returned to Chicago, he contacted the White Way Sign Company. That autumn, he had them paint "Nickey" on one of the side walls of the dealership with the "K" reversed. Immediately, people were coming into the dealership to tell the owners that their sign was wrong. The strong public response encouraged him to change all of the signs, letterheads, and anything else that showed the dealership's name.

With the exception of the gauges mounted to the steering column, the interior of a 1967 Nickey 427 Camaro was pretty much stock. Most buyers didn't really care what the interior looked like as long as it kept them dry and out of the wind. Their interest tended to lie forward of the firewall.

In the muscle-car world, this is the automotive equivalent to a hand grenade with the pin pulled. Those dual four-barrel carburetors weren't there for show. Their job was to feed the massive 427 V-8 with liberal amounts of ethyl gasoline and fresh air. A set of headers guided the exhaust fumes into the vehicle's wake.

If you drove a muscle car in the 1960s and wanted to fit a set of aftermarket wheels, the Cragar S/S was the wheel of choice. When Nickey Chevrolet dressed up their brutal 427 Camaros, they put a new center cap on the popular Cragar wheel, giving the ground-pounder a certain amount of flash.

This was typical of the kind of attention-getting ideas that Jack would have. Though neither Jack nor E. J. had any experience with motorsports, in 1958 they decided that the "Win on Sunday, Sell on Monday" philosophy might have some merit. Unlike some dealerships that just dipped a toe in the motorsports waters, the crew at Nickey dove into the deep end. They started a proper road racing team, using a 1958 Corvette painted purple and imaginatively called the "Purple People Eater" after the 1958 Sheb Wooley popular hit song.

Salesman and racing enthusiast Lionel Lindheimer was put in charge, and Jim Jeffords was tapped to handle driving duties. Even with Chevrolet "officially" out of racing, Nickey's back door still saw quite a bit of factory assistance, from Zora Arkus-Duntov on down. During the 1958 season, Nickey even campaigned the Corvette SR2 at a handful of races. At the end of the season, the Nickey Purple People Eater had won the 1958 B/Production Championship.

Another motorsports venue that Nickey invested in was stock car racing. During the 1958 season, driver Fred Lorenzen from Elmhurst, Illinois, who would win the Daytona 500 in 1965, competed in USAC in 1958 and '59 and would win the championship while sponsored by Nickey.

The best tires of the day didn't stand a chance against a 427 engine with a heavy foot. Using the stock wheel openings limited the amount of rubber that could be used, meaning a light foot was needed during a launch.

Nickey used long ladder traction bars on the 1969 Chevelle to try to hold the A-body's rear axle on the ground when the gas pedal was buried into the carpet. This was the last year for the graceful lines, as the 1970 Chevelle wore more muscular sheet metal.

Seeing the amount of publicity that racing was bringing to the dealership, Nickey bought a Scarab race car at the end of the 1958 season from Lance Reventlow. It was painted the same shade as the Purple People Eater and was dubbed "Nickey Nouse." By mid-season, E. J. decreed that the car was costing the dealership too much money, and he sold it to Jim Jeffords. But this wasn't the end of Nickey and racing.

Following the success of the Purple People Eater in 1958, Nickey built the Purple People Eater Mk II Corvette in 1959. With Jeffords again at the wheel, and Ronnie Kaplan as mechanic, the new car secured the SCCA B/Production National Championship in 1959.

But as quickly as Nickey had burst onto the racing scene in 1958, by the end of the '59 season, it was gone. Nickey pulled back from racing completely. Yet the glamour of racing had bitten the owners at Nickey hard. When the all-new Corvette debuted in 1963, a ZO6 was prepared for competition. Entered in the

Sebring 12 Hour race with A. J. Foyt and Jim Hurtubise at the wheel, it pulled out of the race at lap 84 with engine trouble. In 1964, the car won its class at Sebring, running 183 laps with Jerry Grant and Skip Hudson sharing driving duties.

In 1963, on A. J. Foyt's recommendation, a Cooper Monaco with a Chevrolet engine was purchased. This car was named the "K-Choo" and competed in a wide range of races, including the season-ending party/race/schmoosfest at the Nassau Speed Week. For 1964, Nickey entered the car in the United States Road Racing Championship series. This was the precursor of the Can-Am race series, and racing at this level was an entirely different scene from the original Purple People Eater campaign. Things took a turn for the worse when Bob Holbert spun his King Cobra into the pits at the track at Kent Raceway, injuring Ron Kaplan, one of Nickey's mechanics. The Stephanis decided to sell off their race car. They weren't getting out of the racing

Just your everyday Nickey 427-cubic-inch V-8. With modest modifications, this engine could produce more than 500 horsepower without breaking a sweat. Huge headers were required to help unleash the tire-melting torque.

It looked good on a 1967 big-block Corvette, so Nickey "borrowed" the Stinger hood for its big-block Chevelle. The front and rear of the scoop were nonfunctional, but the impressive hood made a strong graphic statement. Like "don't even think about it."

Performance cars and vinyl tops usually didn't mix, but the original buyer wanted to put an upscale look on the street. Redline tires were a popular option. They didn't grip any better than a whitewall tire, but at least they didn't look like the rubber on Mom's station wagon.

In the first generation's last year, Nickey had honed the Camaro into a brutal performance tool. With a strong presence both on the strip and the street, the Nickey brand was synonymous with no-compromise performance. *Geoff Stunkard*

business, however; they just became race car sponsors instead of race car owners.

In 1965, Nickey Chevrolet sponsored a car in a deal that would have far-reaching ramifications. At the 1964 Nassau Speed Week, Jack Stephani had gotten to know actor Dan Blocker, "Hoss" from the TV show *Bonanza*. Blocker was a big fan of performance, both on and off the track, and he owned a Genie Mk X USRRC car called the "Vinegaroon." Nickey agreed to sponsor the car, and it did well in competition. But more important, Blocker agreed to become a spokesman for the dealership. This arrangement proved to be very lucrative for Nickey. As luck would have it, Chevrolet was the primary sponsor of *Bonanza*, and the link between Blocker and Nickey proved fruitful for all.

The dealership continued to grow. In 1965, Nickey vice president Don Selieg approached parts

manager Don Swiatek and asked if he thought a performance shop would work. Swiatek said that he felt it would, so Selieg told him that he had 30 days to make it work or he'd be out of a job. The Stephanis didn't want to waste time and money with an endeavor that couldn't contribute to the bottom line, quickly. With that, the body shop was transformed into a speed shop. Success was quick to arrive, and soon Swiatek was the manager of the Hi-Performance Department. Body shop operations were outsourced, and word quickly spread among Chevrolet enthusiasts in the Chicago area that one trip to Nickey would satisfy all of their performance needs. Everything from a window decal to a crate engine was on display and ready for delivery.

Swiatek had four technicians who worked on only high-performance jobs, such as installing performance

The backward "K" was a slick marketing trick that kept the dealership's name in people's minds. That's not a bad thing when these people are thinking of a new car purchase. *Geoff Stunkard*

components and engine swaps. There were more than 20 techs that handled new-car work. Due to the large number of vehicles that Nickey was selling and accepting as trade-ins, there were four off-site reconditioning centers devoted to preparing used cars for resale.

As the 1960s progressed, the muscle car market was quickly expanding. It became clear to the Stephanis that the youth had the desire for a fast car, and the money to make it a reality. When a customer would walk into the showroom to buy a performance car, a salesman would quickly steer the "up" to a car. Any of the sales staff was qualified to handle the sale of a high-performance vehicle. Once the model and color of the car was finalized, the customer was handed over to Don Swiatek. Then the fun began, as Swiatek would work with the customer to have the car outfitted with a wide

Nickey Chevrolet worked on enhancing V-8 engines big and small, including the potent 302-CI in the Camaro Z-28. *Geoff Stunkard*

In the late 1960s, performance enthusiasts who wanted to convey the aura of a winner only had to visit a certain Chevrolet dealership on Chicago's Irving Park Boulevard. Then it was simply a case of signing on the dotted line. Next stop: Milwaukee Avenue on a warm Saturday night. *Geoff Stunkard*

No muscle car was complete without a set of flashy wheels. Surrounded by bias-ply tires that might get 10,000 miles if treated gently, on a Nickey muscle car, they would be fortunate to see midnight intact. *Geoff Stunkard*

range of speed options. Once the final configuration was settled on, the customer would then head over to the finance and insurance department, where he would sign on the dotted line. Thus the monthly payment would cover not only the cost of the vehicle, but all of the performance enhancements as well.

Nickey Chevrolet had another way to get customers into the showroom: fly them in! Nickey would pay for a one-way ticket from anywhere in the United States for a customer who wanted a performance car

unlike any available in their hometown. The customer would board a plane and land in the showroom. Of course, Nickey wouldn't buy a return ticket; the customer either bought a car or walked home. Cross-town rival Grand Spaulding Dodge used the same "tactic" to good effect, spreading the gospel of high-performance beyond Cook County. Many impressionable young men would swing past both Nickey and Grand Spaulding on their way home from school, anxious to see what ground-pounders were sitting on the showroom floors.

Never one to let a sales opportunity slip by, Nickey had observed that in Southern California a fellow named Bill Thomas, who had built the brutally fast Cheetah race car, was available for work. Negotiations ensued, and toward the end of 1966, Thomas ended up being Nickey's West Coast presence. Thomas, who was the force behind the potent 377-cubic-inch monster in the Cheetah, came on board with Nickey.

Chevrolet styling hit one out of the park with the debut of the 1970 Camaro. Performance dealers such as Nickey Chevrolet quickly saw the public's interest in the svelte four-seater and wasted no time in preparing it for street and strip duty. The Camaro used the requisite long hood/short deck proportions necessary for a "proper" pony car.

In the interest of safety, shoulder belts were offered, but they weren't exactly easy to use. Far easier to operate was the beefy Hurst T-Handle four-speed shifter. So rugged and reliable were Hurst's shifters that a missed shift was invariably the fault of the driver. The front seats flat bottom cushions did little to provide lateral support, but they were comfortable for Saturday night cruises.

Part of the deal was to sponsor Dick Harrell, a famed drag racer originally from Carlsbad, New Mexico. Harrell was a true Chevrolet believer, running the Bow Tie long after others had jumped for Ford or Chrysler when General Motors stepped away from racing. A skilled mechanic and blessed with legendary reflexes, he made a huge impact on the genesis of the Funny Car. Harrell did so well driving in the first half of 1966 in the Nickey car that Nickey hired him full-time to pilot the Thomas-built Chevy II drag car. Unfortunately, Nickey and Thomas had a falling out in early 1967, and the drag racing program was shut down for the rest of the year.

Meanwhile, Chevrolet introduced its response to Ford's Mustang, the Camaro, in the autumn of 1966. In Southern California, Dana Chevrolet had installed a 427-cubic-inch engine from a 1966 Corvette into the Camaro, with frightening results. Word quickly got out that the engine compartment of the Camaro, designed to accommodate the externally identical 396, swallowed the bigger engine with ease. At Nickey, Don Swiatek wasted no time slipping a 427/425-hp engine in the little four-seater and Nickey was selling Super Cars. Before you could say four-speed, Swiatek had his four master mechanics handling engine swaps for a line of customers who believed that

Chevrolet's solid-lifter small-block engine was a rev-happy powerplant, and after Nickey would "massage" it, the "Mouse" motor would put most big-blocks on the trailer. Being built on the race-track-bred Z/28 platform, the Nickey Camaro could carve corners with far more élan than a regular muscle car, which tended to wallow through the turns like a drunken cow.

Nickey's "Traction . . . Action!" traction bars were an integral part of the performance package that Nickey developed to maximize grip. The yellow bars would limit the amount of rear-axle-spring deflection under heavy throttle, preventing the dreaded axle hop. A tire that's not bouncing can do its job.

Nickey Chevrolet had "Complete Performance Equipped Cars Delivered to You Ready to Race . . . Ready to Win!" But most of the Rat engine installations in 1967 Camaros were done at Thomas' Anaheim, California, shop. This wasn't a cheap vehicle; a Stage III 427 Nickey/Thomas Camaro cost $5,922, $1,500 more than a new Corvette. Of course, 550 horsepower helped justify the price.

Following the edict that flattery is the best compliment, Grand Spaulding Dodge saw that the hated Nickey was now making these big-block street monsters, and in response, stuffed a 383-cubic-inch engine in the little Dart. Like any retail battle, the performance dealers would "steal" ideas and apply them to best effect in their marketplace. The result would be each dealer trying to one-up the competition with more

Nickey used a modified hood to ensure adequate clearance with the engine. Modeled on a Corvette L88 piece, the bulging engine cover was the most visible indication that this Camaro wasn't quite stock. Like most cars of the era, the full-width bumper was basically just for show. Stylists used bumpers as design elements, not for actually protecting the body.

power, more graphics, and more media coverage. The ultimate winner was the buyer.

In 1968, Nickey and Bill Thomas worked together to present another season of fire-breathing Camaros, with do-it-yourself packages, ranging from the modest Stage I kit for $389 to the full-tilt Stage III, retailing for $1,089. Every Chevy enthusiast looked forward to their letter carrier delivering the Nickey Chevrolet Speed Parts Catalog, a veritable dream list of go-fast goodies. If a part was designed for performance and Chevrolet made it, you could have it sent to your house. Even the $1 cost was refunded with the first order. Such a deal!

As other performance dealers had found out, a well-run performance parts department could contribute seriously to a dealership's bottom line. Between walk-ups and mail-orders, Nickey's Speed Shop in the mid-1960s was pulling in more than $60,000 a month. Tucked away in the basement of the dealership was a cinder-block room called The Vault. Inside were the high-dollar crate engines, long and short blocks, waiting to be installed. One owner of a 1969 ZL-1 Camaro recalls driving his pickup truck to Nickey, walking down into The Vault, choosing three ZL-1 engines, and then loading them into his truck.

As the 1960s were drawing to a close, clouds were starting to gather above Nickey Chevrolet. A number of incidents in 1967 set the stage for trouble, including tax problems, an employee theft ring, financing issues, and the Stephanis' efforts to keep the unions at bay. The latter put Nickey Chevrolet in court when a fired employee sued the dealership and the courts forced Nickey to rehire the salesman.

By 1973, General Motors was knocking on the door, as Nickey was "out of trust," meaning they were selling cars but not paying GM. The corporation was given the "choice" of selling the entire dealership or going bankrupt. In response, Nickey closed the doors in December 1973,

From its aggressive stance to the near-overflowing wheelwells, the 2002 Nickey Camaro exuded menace. Aerodynamics played a huge role in determining the contours of the body, aiding both fuel economy and interior noise levels.

Three numbers that mean so much to Chevrolet performance history. Nickey Chevrolet was one of the first dealers to install the "Rat" engine in the 1967 Camaro, and it takes some hard-core enthusiasts to create a modern version.

What would you do with 1,000 horsepower under the hood? Aim and hang on. Using 427 cubic inches of V-8 and a host of performance modifications, this limited edition vehicle pays homage to Bill Thomas and Nickey Chevrolet.

selling the assets, but not the Nickey name, to Keystone Chevrolet. Today, it's Lynch Chrysler Dodge Jeep.

After Nickey Chevrolet was folded, Jack Stephani, Don Swiatek, and Al Seelig opened a speed shop called "Nickey Chicago" on Milwaukee Avenue. Continuing the performance tradition started at the old dealership, they sold speed parts and installed equipment. Unfortunately, the first gas crisis had arrived, and the last thing most people wanted was a street car that got mileage in the single digits. Business suffered, and in 1977, Nickey Chicago closed.

In its day, Nickey Chevrolet had a higher profile than any other performance dealer. With its successful involvement in a wide range of motorsports, few people weren't aware of the backward "K." Nickey helped spread the gospel of performance from coast to coast.

Wearing modern versions of the classic rough-cast five-spoke wheel, the 2002 Nickey Camaro used the biggest tires possible in a futile attempt to harness the 427-cubic-inch engine. In a nod to the late 1960s, red-lines were used at each corner.

Like the "old" days, the '02 Nickey Camaro started life as an SS model; then enhancements were added. With 1,000 horsepower, the dual exhausts have their work cut out for them. The rear wing was functional, but with that kind of power, the rear tires were still traction-challenged.

# CHAPTER 3

# DANA CHEVROLET

## *EIGHTEEN MONTHS OF FUN*

The roots for Dana Chevrolet grew within one man at Ford, or more specifically at Shelby American: Peyton Cramer. Cramer worked for Ford in the early 1960s in the Ford Division controller's office under Ray Geddes in special vehicle operations. He was tapped by Geddes to go out to Los Angeles to help run Carroll Shelby's operation.

While Shelby was building interesting cars, the business side of the venture needed some help. So each week, Cramer would board an airplane and head to L.A., where he'd help straighten out the operation and turn it into a profitable enterprise. After a year as professional tumbleweed, Geddes asked Cramer to stay out there and become Shelby's general manager. Cramer moved his family to the West Coast and continued to assist Shelby. He worked in the general manager capacity for two years, until mid-1965.

The first dealer to install an L72 427 in the then-new 1967 Camaro, Dana used a hood supplied by a local fiberglass shop. Beneath the hood was a Corvette-sourced big-block V-8, able to transform tires into a pool of rubber in seconds. *Mike Mueller*

Just your basic Corvette 427, just not in a Corvette. The Camaro weighed about the same as the 'Vette, and the performance was similarly spectacular. It was oh-so-easy to get in trouble with a Dana Camaro. *Mike Mueller*

This was fair warning to stoplight competitors. But youth tends to feel unstoppable, and many a small-block driver ended up slinking off with his tail between his legs. *Mike Mueller*

In June 1965, Cramer was replaced as general manager, but he stayed on at Shelby, helping in various ways, such as getting a number of European dealerships up and running to distribute Cobras and GT350s. He was gaining experience in running performance-oriented dealerships, a talent he would put to use in the near future. In early 1966, production of Shelby GT350s began migrating to Ford facilities in Michigan, there was no plan for a successor to the Cobra, and the Ford GT racing program had pretty much run its course.

Cramer saw that Shelby American was going to be changing, becoming more corporate, so he left the organization and approached Ford about becoming an automobile dealer. Cramer recalls that, "Ford said that I had no retail experience. I knew Dick Guldstrand,

While this Dana Camaro has a fairly stock interior, Dana high-performance vehicles were tailored to each buyer, outfitted to fulfill their needs and pocketbook. Really high performance didn't come cheap. *Mike Mueller*

who worked with Chevy, and he suggested that I get in touch with Chevrolet." He found out that a dealer in South Gate, California, in the Los Angeles area, Enoch Chevrolet, had gone broke and was shuttered. Through his wife, Cramer met Paul Dombroski and his wife, Margo, on a Saturday outing at Hollywood Park. Dombroski owned a Mercedes-Jeep dealership in Huntington Park, next to South Gate. He told Dombroski that, "I was interested in getting into the car business, but the only way I knew to get in it was to get a partnership with someone who had retail experience. I mentioned to Paul the Chevrolet deal, so we went to Chevrolet and we were able to get the point. We secured a loan from Bank of America, where Paul was banking with his dealership, and we got

The distinctive fiberglass hood that Dana fit on its Camaros used a set of functional scoops to direct air into the engine compartment and a pair of vents at the trailing edge of the hood to allow heated air to be expelled. *Mike Mueller*

West of the Rockies, 427-equipped Camaros were something of a rarity in 1967, as Dana Chevrolet was the first to equip the Mustang-fighter with Corvette power. *Mike Mueller*

Enoch Chevrolet." This was in the autumn of 1966, and big plans were under way.

It was quickly decided that Dombroski would handle the dealership located at 8730 Long Beach Blvd., now called Dana Chevrolet after the side street next to the building, while Cramer would pursue racing. A racing effort requires facilities, and Cramer bought another dealership, Simpson Buick, at 9735 Long Beach Blvd., when its management moved operations to a new building.

Located a couple of blocks from Dana Chevrolet, it was called Dana Hi-Performance Center. It was a full-service dealership, as long as the needs were for Corvettes and Camaros. It had a showroom, parts, and service departments, everything a "normal" dealership had. To staff it, Cramer approached the very same mechanics that had worked at Shelby's shop. When Ford took the Shelby Mustang program to Michigan, the California employees were out of jobs. Cramer knew them, so he brought them into his shop. This was

Depending on the gear ratio and engine, it was possible to cover the quarter-mile in the 11-second range with a Dana Camaro, right off the Hi-Performance Center's floor. Camaros weren't the only vehicles that Dana "massaged"; Chevelles responded equally well to Dana's performance enhancements. *Mike Mueller*

Unrestored, this Dana Camaro was fitted with a cowl induction system that used shop-built components. Most performance cars led hard lives and never saw old age. *Dale Armstrong Collection*

how he was able to get a first-class racing effort up and running in a matter of weeks.

Cramer recalls getting the facility converted into a race shop. "We tore the floor out of the shop, and then poured another one so that it would be perfectly level, so that when we set the race cars up, everything was level. It was the same thing we did at Shelby in the hangers. A lot of these things I picked up from Shelby."

The service department was run by Ken Bilbee, and it offered a full range of performance options for enthusiasts to indulge in. Local Corvette owners were sent a letter dated June 1, 1967, notifying them that the Dana Hi-Performance Center was now open and was "the <u>only</u>

Chevrolet dealer in the Nation with a separate, specialized agency for the sale and service of Chevrolet high-performance automobiles." Keith Collinger, the parts department manager, stocked virtually every performance part Chevrolet made, as well as a full slate of aftermarket parts, such as Hurst shifters, NHRA-approved scattershields, Edelbrock intake manifolds, and engine dress-up bits.

To run the Center, Cramer contacted Dick Guldstrand, who found himself at loose ends when, as Guldstrand recalls, "Mr. Penske decided to let me go. Well, he was mad at me when I crashed his car and got hurt really bad. He wasn't going to pay me until he found out I was going to live." Guldstrand was good

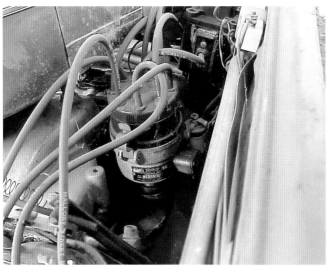

Here's a detailed look at the ignition system used in Dana Camaros. Mallory built rugged high-performance components that many enthusiasts retrofitted onto their cars. *Dale Armstrong Collection*

friends with Zora Arkus-Duntov and Ed Cole, so "I brought a lot to the party." Cramer says, "He acted as the go-between with General Motors and he did all the engineering." Guldstrand was essentially the general manager at the Hi-Performance Center.

As soon as the performance center opened, it was the scene of race car preparation. Guldstrand had extensive experience racing Corvettes, so he and Cramer put together a plan to campaign a Corvette race car. With Sunray Oil from Oklahoma as the primary sponsor, the '67 Corvette coupe, fitted with an L88 427-cubic-inch engine, was race-prepared at the Dana Hi-Performance Center.

Cramer had two drivers for the vehicle: Guldstrand and Bob Bondurant. Then it was off to France to compete in the 24 Hours of Le Mans. The team wanted to go through the engine and replace any parts that they felt couldn't last the entire span of the race, but Chevrolet was adamant that nothing inside the engine would be changed. A failed wristpin, one of the components identified as needing replacement, put the car on the trailer in the 13th hour.

Peter Revson and Bob Bondurant were hired to drive the McLaren race cars for the Dana Chevrolet Team in the 1967 Can-Am race series. When

**DANA HI-PERFORMANCE CENTER**

Southern California has long been recognized as the country's leading innovator in automotive performance development. It is a cultural heritage that stretches back almost as far as the automobile itself. So, it is only natural that when something really new crops up in the performance field it should get its start in this area.

That is the case with Dana Chevrolet's new Hi-Performance Center. Now, for the first time, a major retail automotive agency is offering a separate dealership devoted strictly to high-performance products, service, and development.

Unique in the field, this bold, new concept in modern automotive marketing is the joint effort of Dana Chevrolet's two youthful co-

owners: Paul Dombroski, President, (right in above photo) and Peyton Cramer, Vice-President and Director (left in above photo) of Dana's extensive racing program.

Before forming Dana Chevrolet both men had established successful careers in the automotive and performance fields. As a result they were quick to recognize the need for the type of services the Hi-Performance Center is designed to deliver.

The Hi-Performance Center is much more than just an agency devoted to the selling and servicing of high-performance cars. It goes beyond that by offering the kind of specialized personal service formerly found only in small, out-of-the-way shops. The Center is staffed by specialists chosen for their past experience and knowledge in the performance or racing field.

The Parts Department carries one of the largest stocks of special factory and independently manufactured performance parts in the country.

Over 7000 square feet of space are devoted to the care and feeding that special breeds such as the Camaro, Corvette and others require. The famous Dana 427 Camaros are built here. Another part of the area houses Dana's LeMans Corvette, the Camaro Z-28 sedan racer, and two Dana-built, Chevrolet-powered, Group 7 McLarens which will be campaigned in this year's Can-Am series. This is the only agency where you can get anything from a tune-up to a complete, ready-to-race car.

Dana printed a brochure that highlighted the services that the new Dana Hi-Performance Center was offering. Just visible on the 427 Camaro on the brochure's cover are the traction bars used to minimize rear axle windup under heavy throttle. *Dick Guldstrand Collection*

Dana Chevrolet's co-owners, Peyton Cramer (left) and Paul Dombroski (right), pose by one of the Hi-Performance Center's tire-melting offerings. *Dick Guldstrand Collection*

Bondurant was severely injured in a Can-Am crash at Watkins Glen, Cramer hired Lothar Motschenbacher as the replacement driver to handle the McLaren, and his wife, former race queen Marilyn Fox, as the bookkeeper for the race team. The dealership existed to allow Cramer to go racing.

Members of the public who wanted to go racing, usually from stoplight to stoplight, walked into the Dana Hi-Performance Center with the intent of buying a car that would stomp everyone else. Cramer had just the tool for the job. Don McCain, the sales manager, knew high performance, and he staffed the showroom with like-minded individuals.

The Hi-Performance Center quickly became the Mecca for West Coast enthusiasts. As most racing mechanics put in long hours at the shop getting race cars ready and repairing broken machinery, a crowd often gathered to watch. Peyton Cramer remembers, "We had people coming by at nighttime; we'd have to rope the place off. You know how mechanics are; they'd work 12, 14 hours a day, especially in the race season, so we had to keep the folks back."

The service department stayed busy converting customer-titled cars. The old saw about how fast you

wanted to go was in direct relation to how much money you spent was alive and well at Dana. Many of the cars were bespoke units, as sometimes customers wanted something different. Cramer recalls that "If a buyer wanted Weber carburetors, we gave them Weber carburetors. Whatever they wanted, we supplied."

The main Dana Chevrolet dealership was run by Paul Dombroski, and it handled the full Chevy lineup with the exception of new Corvettes. Those were sold up the street at the Hi-Performance Center. The only vehicles that were sold at the Center were new Dana 427 Camaros, plus new and used Corvettes. Cramer remembers that "Customers with a trade-in would hand over the keys to a salesman at the Hi-Performance Center. He would drive the vehicle to the main dealership, where Paul or the used car manager would appraise it. Then it would be driven back to the Center and be written up as a regular deal."

When Cramer was working at Shelby, he'd gotten a front-row view showing how to ratchet up a vehicle's performance by installing a huge engine. Shelby did it with the installation of the 427-cubic-inch sideoiler engine in the Cobra; Shelby oversaw the installation of the 428-cubic-inch V-8 in the GT500. Peyton Cramer had observed that

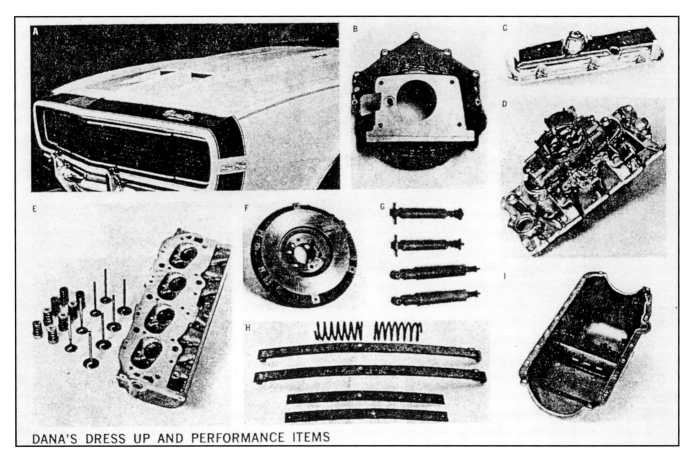

DANA'S DRESS UP AND PERFORMANCE ITEMS

Reading like a wish list for the performance enthusiast, the Dana Hi-Performance Center could supply virtually any part or service, for a price. From weekend cruise machines to full-blown Can-Am cars, Dana did it all. *Dick Guldstrand Collection*

Mechanic/racer Dale Armstrong worked on customer's cars in the daytime, then twisted wrenches on the dealership's race Camaro after hours. Here he focuses his attention on cleaning a camshaft. *Dale Armstrong Collection*

transplanting an engine was a saleable idea, so when he opened his own performance center, he suggested to his crew that a bit of mechanical switcheroo might be possible.

When the Camaro debuted in 1967, it was not offered with a big-block engine until some months later. Don McCain, who followed Cramer from Shelby, was a drag racer, mechanic, and sales manager. He said he took a look at the new Camaro and thought, "Oh, lookie here. I called the parts center up in Oakland to find out what a 427 Corvette engine costs. They said $900. I said, 'You better send me one.' We dropped that puppy in and were selling Dana Camaros for $3,995. He installed a 1966 L72 427/425 Corvette powerplant, and as the engine compartment had been designed to handle the soon-to-be-released 396, the externally identical 427 was a drop-in piece-of-cake."

Driver Dale Armstrong looks back at the camera before launching the Dana Chevrolet Camaro down Orange County Dragway. In the 1950s and '60s, a profusion of drag strips helped the muscle car market grow, as the buyers could flail on the vehicles in relative safety. Today, most of the old drag strips are shopping centers or subdivisions. *Dale Armstrong Collection*

Cramer recalls being behind the wheel of one of his 427 Camaros. "It was really hairy. It wasn't as hairy as a 427 Cobra, because of the weight, but it was probably as close as you could come to driving a 427 Cobra. The power to weight ratio . . . you know those cars weren't that heavy. It got your attention."

As word spread of the potency of the Dana 427 Camaro, two other dealerships took notice and followed the same path to street performance: Nickey Chevrolet in Chicago and Yenko Chevrolet in Canonsburg, Pennsylvania. Magazine articles boasted that the car had too much power for the street, with lurid wheelspin in every gear. The public ate it up.

In the spring of 1968, Cramer remembers that "I had a falling out with Dombroski, and Chevrolet was getting out of racing; they sort of pulled the plug. Dombroski didn't like all the racing I was doing, because I did it all. I was getting all the press and he wasn't getting anything. I put his name on the side of the race cars as co-owner, but I guess that wasn't enough." Cramer decided to sell off his interest in

Dana to Dombroski, as well as all of his racing equipment, including cars and parts, to Carroll Shelby. Ironically, some of Shelby's former employees followed the cars, becoming Shelby employees again. The end was at hand.

Dombroski tried to run Dana by himself, but that quickly fell apart, and the dealership was sold to Cormier Chevrolet. When Dombroski left the facilities, he threw away all of the records, including production information on all of the high-performance vehicles. Hence, today it's very difficult to authenticate a genuine Dana performance car. Cramer went on to own many dealerships, though none of them had the performance bent of the Dana Hi-Performance Center. He sold his dealerships to AutoNation in the 1990s and is now retired.

Eighteen months doesn't seem like a long period of time, but it was long enough to make a strong mark on the performance world. Dana Chevrolet was the result of the right people, with the right experience, being at the right place at the right time.

# CHAPTER 4

# TASCA FORD

## SELLING BY THE CAR LENGTH

It reads like a Hollywood script: Boy works for company, works his way up, company owner skims the money, blows it at the track. Boy gets fed up, strikes out on his own, massive success. Throw in some race cars and titans of industry, bring in some family, more success. The end. Funny thing is, it's the truth, and the story hasn't faded to black yet. Welcome to Tasca Ford.

Bob Tasca Sr. was born in 1928, and when he turned 16, he was busy building his own cars, hopping up the engines, and working on the body. Continuing his love of the automobile, in 1948 he went to work for Harry Sandager at his car lot in Cranston, Rhode Island, painting stripes in the used car lot and whatever the boss wanted him to do. After awhile, Tasca convinced Sandager that he was good for more than menial tasks and came up with an idea.

On the performance car circuit, seeing this on another car was a subtle suggestion to look for trouble elsewhere. Tasca had a well-earned reputation as a builder of very strong running cars, and woe to the driver who ignored that reputation. *Mike Mueller*

For a muscle car, the Torino was a touch on the large size, but it was swoopy looking. Better yet, in Cobra form, it packed a 429-cubic-inch engine. This torque monster did much for moving the Torino out smartly. *Mike Mueller*

Tasca remembers, "He had 70 used cars that were really doing nothing but sitting there, 'cause they needed work. I said, 'I'd like to offer you a proposition: I'll fix those cars; you pay for the parts, I'll pay for the labor. It won't cost you a dime to work on 'em. We'll split the profits, 75 percent for you, 25 percent for me. Sandager thought about it for a while, then said, 'Do it.' Well, I made $26,000 for my share. When Mr. Sandager saw this, he said that I should take over reconditioning." That led to a series of promotions, culminating at general manager.

But there was a problem, as Tasca notes. "I couldn't stand him because he took all the money we made to

the race track. If there were five grand in the bank, he'd take four grand and go to the race track. I used to buy used cars. I couldn't pay for them. I'd have to wait until I'd sold it, then go back and pay the other dealer. That's not the way to do business." Harry Sandager knew how to manipulate money, as he had been a member of the State House of Representatives from 1928 to 1936; then he was elected to Congress from 1939 to 1941. Enjoying the good life was not unusual for Harry Sandager.

Tasca had enough and left Sandager to open his own dealership on November 17, 1953, in Bristol, Rhode Island, at an establishment that had sold just 30

Ordering the Cobra option for the Torino gave the lucky customer 370 horsepower to terrify the neighborhood with. With an 11.3:1 compression ratio, it was mandatory to fill the gas tank with the good stuff. On top of the engine was a 700-cfm Holley that fed fuel into the huge V-8 like you owned stock in Gulf Oil. *Mike Mueller*

For the hard-core lead foot, buying a Torino Cobra meant buying the optional Drag Pak. The result was a dream list of performance components, such as a numerically higher rear axle ratio, forged aluminum pistons, a solid lifter camshaft, remote oil cooler, 780-cfm Holley carb, and more. *Mike Mueller*

cars a year. Tasca came in and sold 126 units in the first two months. But he wanted to be a Ford dealer. He approached Ford Motor Company and asked, "What does it take to become a Ford dealer?" The answer came in the form of a Bristol Ford dealership that had moved only 31 cars a year for the prior three years. When Tasca assumed control, the numbers climbed to 135 cars a year during the first two years. That got Ford's attention.

But things have a way of turning out slightly different than planned, and the catalyst for change was in the form of a Category 3 storm named Hurricane Carol in August 1954. The massive hurricane wiped out Tasca's dealership. He asked Ford for a dealership closer to his home market, near East Providence, Rhode Island. Tasca agreed to step into the dealership on a

With a huge Holley in the engine compartment, it made sense to have a serious fuel pump in the trunk. In a race situation, a stock mechanical fuel pump just couldn't supply enough gas, so it was an easy matter to fit a quality aftermarket electrical fuel pump in the trunk. *Mike Mueller*

With an enormous 429-cubic-inch engine between the shock towers, there wasn't a lot of room left over. Yet a patient mechanic could perform most basic repairs, such as replacing spark plugs and setting valve lash. *Mike Mueller*

trial basis, and by the end of September 1954, he had sold 144 cars. More attention from Dearborn.

As the years passed, Tasca grew into one of the biggest-selling Ford dealerships in the country. Tasca Ford could move plenty of cars out the door, and Ford Motor Company, ever curious, asked Tasca how he sold so many vehicles. Tasca was up-front with the corporation, showing them how he put customers first and foremost. Soon Tasca got to know Henry Ford II. In 1963, "The Deuce" offered Tasca $3 million to work for Ford and teach its employees how to sell. Tasca told Henry that he'd go anywhere for the company, do anything for the company, but wouldn't take a dime. When Ford asked him why he wouldn't take any pay, Tasca told him to just build the right cars. He'd sell them and make plenty of money. Eventually, Tasca

would train over 165,000 Ford employees on the "right" way to do business.

In the early 1960s, Chevrolet was a growing power-house, with a massive share of the market. Or as Tasca put it, "Chevy was kicking the hell out of us. So I said to Henry Ford II in 1962, 'I need your help. I want to build a performance car to compete with Chevrolet, because they're taking all the business.' Ford said 'Do it.' I told Henry what the problem with Ford was. I told him that the people that worked for him didn't understand the car business. They built a car to suit the maker; I sold a car that suited the taker."

As Tasca saw it, Ford was taking the wrong tack to sell performance. "What we needed was a street machine. Ford was in NASCAR building race cars. I

The near-horizontal rear window contributed greatly to the Torino looking slippery. Tipping the scale at 3,700 pounds, it wasn't exactly svelte, but in fact the weight helped the rear tires hook up under heavy throttle. *Mike Mueller*

don't sell race cars, I sell street cars. So I said to Henry, 'You've been spending millions in NASCAR. I don't know how many cars that's sold for you, but I do know this. If you build a street performance car, you'll sell a lot of them.' At the peak, I sold over 100 a month."

Tasca started drag racing in 1962, when he rolled out a 406-cubic-inch Galaxie 500. But Tasca recalls

that "It was not as successful as I wanted because it was too much car. Then I went to a Fairlane, and that went better; as it evolved, it just cleaned house." It was in this period that a young driver named Bill Lawton, a Chevrolet-driving enthusiast, was hanging around the dealership. He test-drove the Galaxie, and the Ford blew his Chevy into the weeds. From then until 1971, he was Tasca's hired gun behind the wheel,

Unlike many serious muscle cars, the initial Cobra Jet, a Tasca invention, was visually subdued. No badging, no stripes, just a modest hood scoop and breathtaking performance. It was actually a bit of a sleeper. *Mike Mueller*

winning championships in many cars, including the 1965 AF/X Mustang Zimmy III.

Chevrolet debuted the Camaro in 1967, and from the beginning, it could be equipped with the potent 396-cubic-inch big block. All Ford had in the competing Mustang was a 390-cubic-inch mill that, frankly, just didn't get the job done. Tasca had seen Mustang sales start to fall off as the impressive Camaro started

pulling enthusiasts into Chevrolet showrooms. This wouldn't do in East Providence. The answer came in the form of a damaged engine. One of his employees had over-revved the engine in a 390-equipped Mustang, so Tasca's high-performance manager Dean Gregson had his crew replace the 390 FE block with a 428-cubic-inch Police Interceptor block. On top of the big piece of iron went a pair of 427 low-riser heads and a 735-cfm Holley carburetor. Inside of the block was a 390 GTA hydraulic camshaft. The resulting engine, called the KR8, would make Ford history.

Except Ford didn't take the engine seriously at first. At least not until the power of the press came onto the scene, in the form of *Hot Rod* magazine. Its technical editor, Eric Dahlquist, heard that Bob

Built for one thing: making power. The beauty of the Cobra Jet was that it was an engine built up from proven parts already on the shelf. It was durable, strong, easy to build and maintain, and best of all, cheap to make. That makes a winning engine in anyone's book. *Mike Mueller*

Ford didn't do anything special for the Cobra Jet interior, putting all of its efforts under the hood. Most performance enthusiasts couldn't have cared less; their interest lay in what happened once the accelerator was buried in the carpet. *Mike Mueller*

All Cobra Jets in 1968 were fastbacks. The first 50 built had consecutive VINs and were painted Wimbledon White. Later cars were available in other colors. *Mike Mueller*

Bob Tasca Sr. used this as his daily driver in 1969. It was pretty much a race car with license plates screwed on. Word spread quickly that running against it wasn't the smartest move. *Geoff Stunkard Collection*

Subtle differences separated the 1969 and 1970 Boss 302s. Besides a different tape graphics package, the taillights were concave in 1969 and flush in 1970. The '69 Boss used four headlights, while in '70, the designers opted for two lamps. *Mike Mueller*

Tasca Sr. had put together some kind of performance engine. Dahlquist had flown into Detroit and picked up one of the first Plymouth Road Runners for a long test drive to New York City. While on the East Coast, he turned it into a family vacation. Imagine how happy the rest of the family was when they pulled up to Tasca Ford. Dahlquist spoke with Tasca and saw the KR8. He took that information back to Los Angeles, where in the next issue of the magazine, he put a "ballot" in, asking readers if they would like to see Ford build the car, then sending the ballot to Henry Ford II. The response was overwhelming.

In the meantime, Tasca used his influence with Henry Ford II to show the corporation what his shop had created. The engineering department was impressed with what they saw, and when the flood of mail from *Hot Rod* readers arrived on the Deuce's desk, the die was cast. Ford engineering was put to work creating a production version of Tasca's engine. Ford released the new engine, dubbed Cobra Jet, in mid-1968 in a run of 50 1968 Mustangs with consecutive VINs. Ford offered it in regular production 1969 Mustangs, Cougars, and midsized Fords and Mercurys. The engine did wonders for Ford's street-performance credibility.

After the Cobra Jet was in production, Tasca remembers telling Henry Ford II, "If we're going to sell Mustangs as performance cars, they're going to need to perform. Henry said, 'Well, what do you want to do?' I told him I want to build a Mustang race car for the track, and a Mustang that races on the street. I

Little was done to the engine of this Tasca Boss 302, as the dealership knew a racing powerplant when it saw one. Though rated at 290 horsepower, in reality, it delivered more like 350. *Mike Mueller*

Stylist Larry Shinoda designed the graphics package on the Boss 302, and it served as a safety function as well as aesthetic purpose. The tape material was reflective, and at night, headlights would cause it to glow. *Mike Mueller*

want a car that's quick enough to beat anything on the highway. The Street Boss was that car." Tasca stuffed a 494-cubic-inch Can-Am engine into a 1969 Boss 429, with staggering results. Wearing street tires and having a closed exhaust system, he could consistently deliver quarter-mile times in the 11-second range. This is what Bob Tasca Sr. drove on the street, looking for a little race action. But word had gotten out about the monster, and Tasca rarely got to flex the car's muscles.

Always aware of performance trends, he saw what Carroll Shelby was doing with Ford components. He became a distributor of Shelby products in the mid-1960s, selling and servicing Cobras and Shelby Mustangs. He would have a longer relationship with Shelby than anyone would imagine.

Any Ford enthusiast would kill to have this badge on the back of his Blue Oval performance car. *Mike Mueller*

Basically stock, the interior of this Tasca 1970 Boss 302 was a business-like place to put the pedal to the metal. *Mike Mueller*

Ford designed a clean-looking wheel for the Boss 302, and its chromed five spokes were an ideal stylistic element in the Boss 302's sporting "look." *Mike Mueller*

In order to meet the SCCA's requirement for racing a production car, at least 6,500 Boss 302s had to be built. When the dust settled, Ford had produced 7,013. *Mike Mueller*

For a dealer to be taken seriously in the performance market in the 1960s, it had to have more on the table than just fast cars for sale. Service and parts played a huge role in expanding a dealership's influence in enthusiast markets. Not every person who walked into a dealership was there to buy a hot car, but it was a common practice to modify customers' cars to suit their performance needs, as well as to supply them with over-the-counter parts to install themselves. In the late 1960s, Tasca was selling over $100,000 a month in performance parts alone.

He devised a clever system for selling parts, based on car lengths. Someone would come into the dealership and Tasca would ask, "How bad did you get beaten last weekend?" The car owner might say "two car lengths." Tasca would reply, "This package will give you four car lengths."

Tasca was always building performance cars at the dealership, then testing them at a local drag strip. He knew what combination of parts would work, and by how much. He could deliver consistent car lengths, for a price. If the car didn't deliver as promised, Tasca's policy was that the customer got the package for free. In all his years in the performance field, he never gave a package away.

Tasca Ford had invested considerable resources to compete on the drag strip, and few dealers competed at this level. The lightweight Mustang was a good platform for performance modifications. *Geoff Stunkard Collection*

With its Holman-Moody-built engine, the Mystery 9 1966 Mustang quickly made obsolete its name as it broke out of the 9-second range and ventured into the 8-second club. This was one way-fast car. *Geoff Stunkard Collection*

With Bill Lawton behind the wheel, the altered Mystery 8 Mustang was a terror on any drag strip it ran on. With the tires of the day, the hardest part of drag racing was getting the power to the ground, not up in the air in the form of smoke. *Geoff Stunkard Collection*

Donald Frey (left) and Bob Tasca Sr. gaze at the silver bowl awarded to Tasca's 505 Mustang by *American Rodding* magazine. This refined version of a 2+2 Fastback Mustang was picked as America's "Perfect Performance Car" in 1965. *Mike Mueller Collection*

Tasca used the racing program as a training ground for his service mechanics. They got used to working under pressure, finding a problem and fixing it as quickly as possible, all important attributes in motorsports competition. Tasca went to the track to win, and that meant that the entire team had to function on all cylinders. Two stalls in the service department were dedicated race car areas, and with the long service hours that Tasca employed, 7 a.m. to midnight, there were always plenty of hands to twist wrenches.

By 1971, the writing was on the wall. A combination of factors, especially rising insurance rates and the need for auto manufacturers to build vehicles that could meet the increasingly stringent emission regulations, would shove the performance car off of the stage. Tasca was reluctant to compete on the dragstrip in a vehicle that wasn't powered by gasoline. He felt that a production-car dealership should compete with street-type cars, not vehicles fueled by alcohol or nitro. Tasca said he felt that "If I can't sell

It's April 1967, and the executives at Tasca Ford get ready to greet racing legend Mario Andretti, who was on hand to help celebrate the Mustang's third anniversary. The 1968 Mustang next to the street-legal GT40 is the car that became the Cobra Jet prototype. *Mike Mueller Collection*

Gordon Carlson, a Tasca customer, wanted to race his 406 Galaxie. Bob Tasca Sr. felt that sponsoring Carlson could pay off in exposure, so Tasca started down the performance path. In the foreground are Bob Tasca's sons, Bob Jr. (left) and Carl. *Mike Mueller Collection*

it on Monday, I don't want to race it on Sunday. I'm not in the business to win races; I'm in the business to sell cars."

Performance continues to motivate Tasca Ford. Currently, three generations of Tascas work in the various dealerships, and Bob Tasca III actively campaigns a Shelby Mustang Funny Car developing 3,500 horsepower. In 2007, Shelby and Tasca announced a collaboration in which Tasca would become the East Coast headquarters for Shelby American, including vehicle modifications. It's clear that performance helped propel Tasca to the front ranks of the performance field, and they have no intention of pulling back.

Talk about a halo car. Few dealerships ever saw a GT40; much less were able to display one. But Bob Tasca was a friend of Henry Ford II, and with friends like that, anything was possible. *Mike Mueller Collection*

**Below:** Chevrolet driver Al Oakes was tired of his Corvette being beaten by Tasca Ford's 406 Fairlane. So in May 1962, he arranged to "swap" cars with the Tasca crew so that Oakes raced in the Fairlane and one of the Tasca drivers handled the Corvette. The Fairlane won, again. *Mike Mueller Collection*

# CHAPTER 5

# BALDWIN-MOTION

## *HELL ON WHEELS*

It started in Brooklyn. Bedford-Stuyvesant, actually, at a Sunoco gas station in the late 1950s. Joel Rosen, born in 1939 and bred in Brooklyn, didn't grow up with cars in his family. His parents didn't have an automobile until Joel was 16. He learned to drive in a 1947 Plymouth, and when he took his first driving test, he crashed into a telephone pole and bent the front axle. Yet he learned which end of a wrench to hold while serving in the U.S. Air Force in the late 1950s as a reciprocating engine mechanic.

Upon returning to civilian life, he was approached by the owner of the Sunoco station on the corner of Albany and Atlantic Avenues in Brooklyn to join as a junior partner. In his spare time, Joel tended to gravitate toward racing, first in a straight-axle 1958 fuel-injected Corvette. After wiping it out in a hill climb race, he ended up with another Fuelie 'Vette, a 1962. More racing ensued.

When Motion Performance was involved, this badge was as discreet as it got. Often Motion-prepped cars wore flamboyant paint and wild body mods.

Buyers wanting a performance car could approach Motion Performance directly or head into Baldwin Auto Company, the local Chevrolet dealership. Their order would be processed, money taken, and soon the lucky customer would own a terror for the street. *Courtesy of Motion Performance*

Motion Performance would work on anything with a reciprocating engine, including an Iso Grifo. Equipped with a large Chrysler engine in an Italian body, it was an interesting blend of American brute power and svelte European design. *Courtesy of Motion Performance*

When the 1963 Corvette hit the street, Rosen was in love. Buying a fuel-injected coupe, he flogged it at drag strips throughout the area, as well as using it as his daily driver between his home on Long Island and the station. The 'Vette was known affectionately as "The Skunk," thanks to its dark Daytona Blue exterior with white racing stripes.

In 1963, Rosen convinced his partner that the station needed a Clayton chassis dynamometer and an oscilloscope. There were only a couple of dynamometers in the entire Northeast, and using it in conjunction with a Sun Diagnosis oscilloscope allowed Rosen to fine-tune an engine under load. It was this same year that a new sign went up in front of the station, "Motion Performance."

Rosen was an early convert to electronic ignition systems, and he used a capacitive discharge system called the Motion EI 5 CD. He "borrowed" the name for his own business. The editor of *Cars* magazine, Martyn Schorr, wrote an article about a Corvette that Rosen had built, and the two men hit it off. Schorr would figure prominently in the future of Motion Performance and the creation of Baldwin-Motion.

Word got out that this kid knew how to make a car really run, and business was good. But the neighborhood wasn't, and when, as Rosen puts it, "they started shooting back instead of talking back," he was out of there. It was 1966, and he pulled stakes and headed out to Long Island's Sunrise Highway in Baldwin, New York.

Rosen and partner Jack Geiselman opened in the new facility, and Motion Performance continued to grow. After about six months, Geiselman didn't want to do it anymore, so Rosen bought him out. Marty Schorr was now handling the advertising needs of Motion, and word was getting around about the cars rolling out of Long Island.

Joel continued to work on customers cars', using nearby Baldwin Chevrolet as a source of factory parts, and became friends with the parts manager there, John Mahler. Mahler helped Rosen put together a presentation for a program that Rosen and Schorr had been planning. Rosen proposed an arrangement to Baldwin

Shortly after Charlie Snyder got to Vietnam, he was killed by a mortar round. The car sat in his mother's garage until Joel Rosen and John Mahler inquired about the possibility of running the car in Charlie's memory. *Randy Leffingwell*

Chevrolet's owner that would allow customers to buy a new car at the dealership, then have it sent down the street to Motion Performance, where it would be outfitted with the exact speed equipment the buyer wanted, while still being a new car with a warranty.

Strictly a Mom-and-Pop dealership, Baldwin Chevrolet was run by Ed Simonin, son of the founder August "Gus" Simonin, and David Bean. Baldwin was the kind of dealership that catered to the sale of mainstream vehicles such as the Impala and Chevelle. They wouldn't know a high-performance muscle car if it ran them over. But Rosen convinced them that if they would supply the cars that he would then set up for performance, Baldwin

Chevrolet would become famous. Strangely enough, that's pretty much what happened.

With the introduction of the Camaro in 1967, Joel Rosen and Marty Schorr were ready to put Rosen's idea into action. Baldwin gave Rosen a couple of vehicles to build prototypes and agreed to pick up the advertising bills. Rosen was given anything he needed: engines, parts, anything. This was due partly to John Mahler in the parts department, who was, as Rosen remembers, "a high-performance fanatic like me. He was instrumental in, number one, helping to sell the program, and then in getting the dealership ready and keeping it stocked as we went along with the parts that were necessary."

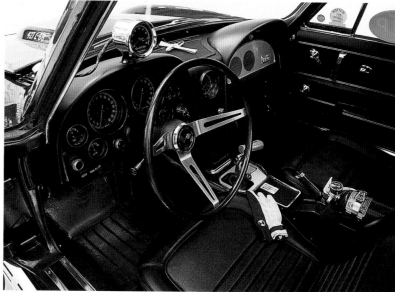

Ko-Motion's original owner, Charlie Snyder, was from Astoria, New York. He purchased the car to participate in AHRA-sanctioned drag races where it would run the quarter-mile in 11.5 seconds at 124 miles per hour. *Randy Leffingwell*

**Left:** This is probably the first L88 engine to land in private hands. When the Corvette's original L71 427 engine passed on, Joel Rosen installed an L88 that he had just gotten from Chevrolet. This powerplant was designed for the race track and could generate well over 500 horsepower. *Randy Leffingwell*

With John Mahler at the wheel, the Ko-Motion Corvette ran the quarter-mile in a best time of 10.74 seconds. It was then returned to Grace Snyder's garage. *Randy Leffingwell*

While the first owner drove it on the road, the fitment of a tow bar and freewheeling hubs hinted that the car saw duty on the drag strip. With a 4.56:1 rear axle ratio, it could cover the quarter-mile in 11.4 seconds, tripping the lights at 120 mph. *Randy Leffingwell*

When an engine breathes through a 950-cfm Holley carburetor, chances are good that it's a barely contained bomb. An expensive bomb, this Motion Camaro stickered for a lofty $9,330. More than 500 horsepower lived within the iron block 427-cubic-inch engine, and they liked nothing better than to come out and play. *Randy Leffingwell*

The prototype car Rosen assembled was a 1967 Camaro that he equipped with a 427-cubic-inch engine. Then he approached Baldwin Chevrolet again, and as Rosen recalls, "I sold him on the idea that we couldn't do this (the street car program) unless we built a race car, because if you don't race, people aren't going to believe the cars are fast. People [who] bought my vehicles weren't the Yenko-type people, geared to road racing, because that's what he did. I thought we needed to do a drag vehicle." So Rosen built his drag car, filling the engine compartment with one of the first L88 427-cubic-inch engines released through the GM parts network.

73

Sourced from an Oldsmobile, the rear wing added a bit more flash to an already very flashy Motion Camaro. This was the most heavily optioned Camaro that Motion built, and rowing the Hurst shifter down the drag strip made every run a high-drama event. *Randy Leffingwell*

The original owner, Roberto Schneider Irigoyen, specified "no tach" when he ordered the car. He wanted a hood-mounted tach, but it wasn't possible to get it installed. Virtually every other option available was fitted to the car though, and it was destined to roar down the deserted roads of Mexico. *Randy Leffingwell*

Motion Performance's shop was on the edge of town, and when heading toward the neighboring town, a long straight stretch of road was available to test cars. Rosen remembers that "the Nassau County cops on patrol were hot-rod fans, and they would look the other way when they heard me running cars, sometimes with open pipes."

With success on the track, and *Cars* magazine sponsoring the race car and writing about Motion Performance, performance part makers such as Edelbrock, Holley, and Hooker Headers were soon on board to supply go-fast goodies. Motion was stuffing 427 engines in Camaros, Novas, Biscaynes, Corvettes, and Chevelles. Camaros were ordered from Baldwin Chevrolet in RPO L78 396/375-horsepower guise. The standard big-block engine was pulled and replaced

The new-for-1970 body of the Chevelle boasted a beefy, street-fighter look, and the Motion Phase III 454 had the goods to back up the looks. Tipping the scale at almost two tons, the Chevelle wasn't the lightest Chevy that Motion Performance worked on, but with 500 horses beneath the tall hood, merging onto a highway wasn't much of an issue. *Randy Leffingwell*

**Right:** A Motion Chevelle was a comfortable place to abuse pavement. With power windows and full instrumentation, the driver wasn't exactly roughing it. When the open highway was in the windshield, pulling back on the black-knobbed handle activated the Hone overdrive, dropping the final drive ratio from 4.88:1 to 3.70:1. *Randy Leffingwell*

**Below:** When any automobile is equipped with 4.88:1 rear axle gears and 500 horsepower, the tires are pretty much DOA with any press of the accelerator pedal. Potential rivals would come up and see the "Motion" emblem on the rear bumper, and if they had a hint of a brain, they'd look elsewhere. *Randy Leffingwell*

The Motion GT Phase III was not a car for introverts. With its vibrant two-tone finish, traveling under the radar was pretty much out of the question. The dramatically sloping rear window increased interior room and improved the aerodynamics. With its big-block engine, it was a case of carrying a really big stick.

Except for the air cleaner and valve covers, the Motion GT Phase III's engine compartment looked stock. The difference was inside the engine, as the 454-cubic-inch mill was delivering well over 500 horsepower. It didn't take a lot of throttle to scare yourself to death.

Widening the wheelwells and filling them with huge tires didn't solve the inherent traction problems of putting the 454's massive torque to the ground. Joel Rosen designed the body modifications, then local body shops would create the final product.

It only took a moment's inattention to sear a leg on the huge side exhaust pipes. A stereo was superfluous, as the snarl from the exhaust would drown out any sound system. Fixed and covered headlights gave the Motion GT Phase III a European flavor, while ensuring an effective light pattern at any speed.

with a well-tuned 427 crate engine. The result was about 450 horsepower melting the rear tires. Additional options were available, anything the client wanted.

The crew at Motion Performance numbered about 20, between the mechanics in the shop and the front office staff, and they were never hurting for work. Schorr kept the Baldwin-Motion name front and center in enthusiast magazines, and the publicity and advertising paid off.

Except for the demo cars that Joel Rosen kept handy, virtually every car Baldwin-Motion built was a bespoke vehicle. Customers with money burning holes in their pockets had three ways to put a Baldwin-Motion ground-pounder in the garage. The first way was via mail order. Motion Performance mailed hundreds of catalogs to potential buyers around the world, especially to American military forces fighting in the Vietnam War. Often, servicemen would order and pay for a vehicle while overseas, then upon their return to the States, swing by Baldwin, New York, to pick up the car.

Another route to owning a Baldwin-Motion automobile was to actually go to Motion Performance and

talk with Joel Rosen. There were always a couple of Motion cars on the premises, and any wavering by a potential customer was banished when Rosen would take them for a test drive. He would write up the order depending on the wants and needs of the customer, then take the order to Baldwin Chevrolet.

The third path to ownership would be to walk into Baldwin Chevrolet and ask to speak with someone about a Baldwin-Motion car. When the Baldwin-Motion partnership was in its infancy, some of the sales staff were afraid of losing a commission, so they would steer customers toward a 396/375 Camaro rather than send them down to Motion Performance. The owners of Baldwin Chevrolet soon found out about the practice and decreed that anyone looking to buy a Motion product would be taken care of by the dealership owners directly. That took care of the problem. Rosen noted that "customers that came to me tended to buy more performance equipment, as I spoke their language."

In 1968, Oldsmobile was awarded Car of the Year by *Cars* magazine for the 4-4-2, so Schorr and Rosen were invited to Oldsmobile headquarters in Lansing, Michigan, to tour the facilities and talk about bringing

This GSX's first owner wanted to shake things up even more with a visit to the skilled hands at Motion. Buick was trying to shake the staid image from decades of "doctor's cars." Saturn Yellow was a standard GSX color, and it wasn't for the shy. *Geoff Stunkard*

As was Motion's modus operandi, the stock engine was removed, a replacement block was installed, and a score of speed components were bolted on, including a huge three-barrel, 980-cfm Holley carburetor. Motion Performance created only two Buicks, both of them "built" cars, meaning they were post title, or already privately owned. *Geoff Stunkard*

Buick traditionally equips its cars with comfortable interiors, but the crew at Motion wanted to make it a bit more velocity-friendly. A hidden control panel beneath the dash controlled the ignition, alarm, fuel pumps, and brake lights. *Geoff Stunkard*

some of the Baldwin-Motion magic to Olds. To that end, Motion Performance was given two 4-4-2s, one a W-30, the other a W-31. Also thrown in the deal were two Oldsmobile tow vehicles. A dealer close to Motion Performance, Mack Markowitz Oldsmobile of Hempstead, New York, was approached, a deal was struck, and the cars were set up for racing.

Everything was progressing smoothly when the mechanics at the Oldsmobile dealership convinced the front office that they didn't need these Motion Performance guys; they could do just as well on their own. When the Markowitz Olds folks rolled up in their first car, it wasn't running right, and they showed Rosen the car. He said, "I never built that car; this is the first thing I've heard about it. I was pissed off, I cut their advertising, I cut off their relationship with Oldsmobile. The program disappeared. It could have been a tremendous thing."

Upscale, in a sporty fashion, the GSX offered superior materials and excellent build quality. Add a dose of Motion's magic and the speedometer suddenly gets a full-range workout. *Geoff Stunkard*

Of course this GSX needed twin fuel pumps. With a huge 455-cubic-inch engine and a thirsty Holley carburetor, it was all the pumps could do to keep an acceptable pressure in the fuel supply line. It helped that ethyl was 33 cents a gallon. *Geoff Stunkard*

That's not a Buick rear axle beneath the body. Motion knew what a 12-bolt Chevrolet axle would take, and with the power the boys at Motion coaxed from the GSX, the rear end needed to be very stout. *Geoff Stunkard*

The word "subtle" has never been in Joel Rosen's vocabulary, and the 1973 Motion 454 Camaro is proof. With its wild two-tone paint, bulging hood, and aggressive stance, the F-body from Motion was like a Camaro on steroids—very strong steroids.

Joel Rosen continued to campaign drag cars sponsored by *Cars* magazine under the Motion Performance banner from 1967 through 1972. Besides using the quarter-mile as a research tool, it kept the Motion Performance name in front of the very enthusiasts that Rosen was courting. These cars were fierce competitors, and held multiple NHRA and AHRA national championships. The engine of choice was the huge 427-cubic-inch V-8 until 1970, when the even bigger 454-cubic-inch engine was modified for action.

Being Motion Performance cars, the line between drag strip and street was blurred with the road versions, especially when customers ordered the top-of-the-line Phase III package. Rosen put his money where his mouth was when he stated, "We think so much of our Phase III Supercars that we guarantee they will turn at least 120 mph in 11.50 seconds or better with an M/P-approved driver on an AHRA or NHRA-sanctioned drag strip." In all of his years doing business, Rosen never paid out a dime.

Baldwin-Motion cars came in two flavors, SS and Phase III. The SS cars were given upgrades according to the buyer's needs and budget, such as starting with a Z/28 Camaro and installing an LS-6 454 engine. The Phase III cars, while street legal, were little more than race cars with a license plate frame.

The full range of Chevrolet passenger cars were fair game for the Motion treatment, cars such as the Camaro, Chevelle, Corvette, Vega, and Nova. Stuffing a Rat engine in a lightweight Vega created a monster. Rosen didn't care much for the Vega package due to the lack of traction. Fewer than 100 units were built during the entire span of Motion Performance's involvement.

The success of Motion Performance allowed Rosen to indulge in the creation of an occasional, limited edition run of cars, such as the Motion GT, Maco Shark, Spyder, and the Manta Ray. These vehicles started life as Corvettes, but Rosen had transformed them into wild, powerfully stylistic rolling

Better living through cubic inches: With 454 of them in the Motion Camaro's engine compartment, it would take a blind fool to pull up next to this beast on a Saturday night and really plan on winning. Rosen guaranteed his cars would develop stupid speed on cue; he never had to give a dime back.

While the bundle of chrome tubes flowing out from beneath the fender looked impressive, what they did for the Motion Camaro's performance was nothing short of staggering. These road rockets would spin their tires in all four gears if that was a driver's wish.

statements. Various bits and pieces from other vehicles were used on the Motion cars, such as Mustang Mach 1 mirrors and Charger gas caps.

Rosen would rely on local body craftsmen to build what he designed. He feels that building the special cars allowed him to stretch artistically. "I was able to experiment with all this stuff, knowing that sooner or later I'd sell it." Today he laments that he didn't hang onto some of the cars. But as he says, "I had to sell this stuff to pay the bills. It was my business."

Eventually, Baldwin Chevrolet was sold and became Williams Chevrolet, then sold again to become

With its glinting Cragar S/S wheels full of sticky rubber, a '73 Motion 454 Camaro is all about trolling for trouble. Buyers could spring for a Hone overdrive, allowing the quick muscle car to be a fast muscle car. Virtually any option was possible; just bring money . . .

Having this badge on your car was a real source of pride, as well as confidence that any challengers at a stoplight encounter would continue to see this view of the Camaro.

Lyons Chevrolet. That incarnation closed its doors in 1974, forcing Joel Rosen to look to other local Chevrolet dealerships to supply him with new cars.

Things progressed until 1974, when a *Car Craft* magazine published article, "King Kong Lives on Long Island," about the 454 Motion Super Vega hit the newsstands. This caught the eye of the Environmental Protection Agency, who took issue with the removal of the stock emission equipment and responded with a fine of $50,000 for each car built. They descended onto Motion Performance with a cease and desist order, effectively shutting down business as usual.

The twin black stripes on the huge hood looked like dual landing stripes, but beneath the swoopy fiberglass was essentially a slightly de-tuned race engine for the street. Motion cars were expensive for the time; the adage asking how fast you wanted to go was answered by how much money you wanted to spend. Motion buyers got their money's worth.

In 1975, Rosen settled with the government for $500 and following the particulars in the EPA and Department of Justice documents. But even that didn't stop the former racer from building high-performance vehicles. The difference between then and before was that the new cars were labeled "For Export" or "For Off Road Use Only."

In the early 1980s, Rosen built a number of Motion IROC Camaros and Monte Carlos, including his personal vehicle, a 1987 Motion IROC SS Aero Coupe that used a Monte Carlo as the basis. It was equipped with a supercharged 350-cubic-inch V-8, that, when the nitrous bottle was kicked in, developed around 500 horsepower.

At the 2005 SEMA show, Joel Rosen and Marty Schorr unveiled the latest offerings from Motion Performance. Most notable was a 1969 Camaro, massaged to become a Baldwin-Motion Camaro SuperCoupe, equipped with a Kinsler-injected aluminum 540-cubic-inch V-8 producing in excess of 600 horsepower. With the sophistication of today's on-board computer systems, Rosen is able to extract massive horsepower while maintaining socially responsible emissions. At the 2006 Barrett-Jackson auction in Scottsdale, the SuperCoupe sold for a staggering $486,000. Striking to see, and brutal to drive, the SuperCoupe encompasses all of the special qualities that Joel Rosen has built into his vehicles ever since he worked at a corner gas station in Brooklyn.

# CHAPTER 6

# GRAND SPAULDING DODGE

## WE CAN BUILD IT FOR YOU!

The term Windy City refers to Chicago's politicians, but over the years, the weather has done its share to shape careers. Norm Kraus grew up pumping gas at his father's service station at the northwest corner of West Grand Avenue and North Spaulding Avenue in Chicago, Illinois, a predominantly blue-collar neighborhood. That's how Grand Spaulding Dodge started. Really. As a youth, Kraus endured the Windy City's heat and cold to fill up customers' cars.

Like so many teenagers following World War II, he was in love with performance. However, he didn't want to pump gas and twist wrenches. He sold his father, Harvey, on the idea that having a couple of cars wearing *For Sale* signs on a portion of the station property might bring in a few extra dollars. It was 1948, and Norm with his brother Lenny grew skilled in the art of selling used cars under the banner Grand Spaulding Motors.

Grand Spaulding Dodge would tune each muscle car it sold on one of the Clayton dynos in the service department. That would put a fine edge on the engine. Of course, when the car was in need of a tune-up, where else would you take it?

From a stylistic standpoint, the 1968 Dart didn't win any awards, but as a lightweight platform into which to shoehorn a big engine, it picked up plenty of trophies.

B usiness was good. So good that in 1951, they bought the lot next door, filled it with cars for sale, strung some lights over them, and moved even more metal. Their father's service station handled needed repairs, and in 1957 the brothers decided to specialize in vehicles that leaned toward sporting. The circumstance behind the decision was unusual; an insurance adjuster came into the lot with a 1956 Chevrolet convertible that had seen better days. He put an ad in the paper saying "1956 Chevy convertible, V-8, stick. Call Mr. Norm." The phone rang off the hook.

Norm told Lenny, who was out buying cars to sell on their lot, "That's it, no more regular cars. Buy every car with a V-8 and a stick that you can find." Big engines and manual transmissions stood out from the normal used car lot offerings: hot Oldsmobiles, Buicks, and Chryslers, anything that wore a whiff of

performance. The brothers approached other area dealers while looking for performance cars. Most of these dealers welcomed the chance to unload them to the Kraus brothers. Other dealers couldn't or wouldn't pursue performance, content to sell luxury or thrift. The Kraus brothers felt otherwise, advertising the fact in tiny, two-line ads in the *Chicago Sun Times*, encouraging performance-hungry readers to "Call Mr. Norm." The moniker stuck, and sales were steady.

As the 1950s wound to a close, a regional Dodge rep looking to sign up franchisees would stop by the lot periodically and talk to the brothers about becoming a Dodge dealership. He would be told thanks but. . . . The Kraus brothers were underwhelmed with the look of Dodge vehicles in the early 1960s, and they told the rep that. The rep assured them that Chrysler had gotten a new designer, and that in the near future, Dodge would

Looks right at home, doesn't it? When Norm Kraus suggested to the factory that he'd like to have some Darts with big-block engines, Detroit told him that it couldn't be done. Phooey, or words to that effect later, Grand Spaulding had made it a reality.

have some good-looking vehicles. Finally, they acquiesced, signing up in the fall of 1962.

So the Kraus brothers were Dodge dealers. Granted, they didn't have a showroom or proper service facilities, but they had an order pad. True to what had gotten them there, performance cars were stressed. The entire first order from the factory was Max Wedge cars, a thinly disguised racing engine for the street. Kraus figured that he'd get one car now, maybe two later. He didn't realize that Max Wedge cars were batch-built. Imagine Kraus' surprise when a line of transporters pulled up in a blizzard with the entire order. The cars were rolled off

*Continued on page 90*

Because there were no 440 emblems, Grand Spaulding left the 383 emblems in place. Imagine the surprise of a street race competitor when the big 440 lit up and hurled the diminutive Dart down the road.

Slab sides, crisp roofline, and simple rear treatment speak budget car, but by adding a 440-cubic-inch V-8, Grand Spaulding transformed the 1968 Dart into a feared street brawler. Bumblebee stripes around the tail were a product of the times, when wild graphics were expected.

Okay, maybe cutting away part of the inner wheelwells to supply clearance for the headers isn't the tidiest way to solve a big engine in a small compartment equation, but it got the job done. Few expected these cars to see more than one or two winters before they would be used up and discarded.

The Dodge Dart was designed to be a thrifty, simple car, and the interior showed that spirit. The chrome-plated center console bisecting the front bucket seats gave the subdued interior a bit of flash. Pushing the accelerator to the floor provided a lot more flash.

Using letters in the parts bin, Grand Spaulding created the GSS moniker, meaning Grand Spaulding Sport. But casting 440 emblems would have cost more money than Norm Kraus wanted to spend, so he went with the factory 383 logos.

In the 1960s, there were few dealerships that invested more in pursuing enthusiasts than Chicago, Illinois-based Grand Spaulding Dodge. In Mopar circles, nothing beat a performance car with this coveted dealer decal.

Most drivers, glancing in their rearview mirrors, would see that unassuming front end and ignore it. They probably wouldn't believe it was the same car that, seconds later, would suck their doors off. Sometimes trolling with a sleeper is a lot of fun.

With the wraparound front bumper, the Road Runner for 1971 wore a more curvaceous body than in prior years. The low nose and raised rear haunches gave the muscle car an aggressive look, as if it were ready to spring.

*Continued from page 87*

of the transporters and parked in the lot, and then sawhorses were set up surrounding them to form a corral to make it look like this kind of collection of high-performance machinery was an everyday occurrence. Kraus got on the phone and talked with other used-car dealers and each of them agreed to keep one car at their facilities. Eventually, all of the Max Wedge cars were sold.

In the spring of 1963, the old gas station was torn down and a three-car showroom was built, yet service facilities were lacking. Local buildings were pressed into duty until a "real" service department could be constructed. Once they were in place, things started picking up steam. The Kraus brothers had chosen to stress performance cars, and Grand Spaulding Dodge stocked primarily "muscle." With Lenny in the "back" of the store, handling the promotion, budgets, sales, and ordering, Norm was the highly visible "face" of Grand Spaulding Dodge, his smiling visage gracing ads for years. Norm and Lenny studied other dealerships like a bookie studies the ponies, seeing what would work, or not. One dealer might be tops at used-car sales, while another

With the gradual increase in the size of engines, Detroit "grew" the size of the engine compartment. To accommodate the bigger engine room, the rest of the vehicle tended to grow. Then, to haul the bigger, heavier body around, a larger engine was needed. To handle the increase in the size of the engine . . .

Nail the throttle, and the hood scoop would pop up, directing cooler, denser air into the air cleaner. Engines tend to generate more power with cooler air, so the huge Hemi beneath the long hood appreciated the infusion of cold air. It didn't hurt that the scoop looked cool.

Strobe stripes on the huge C-pillars helped break up the large expanse of sheet metal. The forward tilt of the stripes gave the car a visual energy, even when sitting still.

The 426 Hemi made its last appearance in the 1971 Road Runner. The huge performance engine didn't have a future in a world of increasingly strict emission regulations and rising insurance rates. But in '71, it could still melt tires like nobody's business.

If packing a 440 V-8 was rolling excess in 1968, what kind of rolling insanity is a Dart with a 572 Hemi? Stupid, crazy, brutally fast, the latest GSS Dart is more of everything in one handsome package.

excelled at leasing. The Kraus brothers cherry-picked the techniques of the competition and created what would be the biggest Dodge dealership on Earth. It didn't happen by accident.

After the service facilities were erected, a second-hand Clayton Chassis Dynamometer was installed to allow the technicians to fine-tune an engine. This allowed each performance car to be set up prior to delivery to a buyer, as well as performing tune-ups under load. Before a new performance car would roll out of the dealership, it went on the dyno, where the rejetted carburetor and recurved distributor were dialed in under simulated track conditions. This kind of service might have been considered somewhat antisocial, but customers flocked to the West Side dealership.

Able to swallow small pets, the hood scoop on the 1968 GSS Hemi Dart grabs huge chunks of air to feed the all-aluminum 572-cubic-inch Hemi engine. Only 40 of these monsters are being built. Bring cash, lots of it.

Topped by a pair of huge carburetors, the all-aluminum 572 Hemi fills the engine compartment to near-overflowing. Yet the inner wheelwells didn't suffer as they did in the old days. The lift-off hood makes accessing the top of the engine a snap.

Recognizing that the buyers of performance cars were members of the growing Baby Boomer Generation, Kraus started the "Mr. Norm's Sport Club." Buyers of a performance car were automatically enrolled, and benefits included window decals, license plate frames, a monthly newsletter, and a subscription to *Drag News*. That last item was a solid indicator of the Mr. Norm Grand Spaulding Dodge philosophy; fast cars on the street and the track. In an effort to appeal to younger buyers, Kraus put on an open house with bands such as "The Buckinghams" playing popular music in the service department.

Potential buyers were reading about the new crop of muscular cars rolling out of Detroit in the buff magazines, and they'd approach other Dodge dealers about getting their hands on one. Virtually every other dealer had zero performance cars in

stock, but they'd tell the customer that they could order one.

When an "up" would hit the showroom with cash in the pocket, the last thing the customer wanted was to wait for his or her dream car to come down the assembly line; he or she wanted it now! So the dealer would call Grand Spaulding Dodge about buying a performance car from them. Mr. Norm's response was "Hell no!" If they want a real performance car, they can drive to Grand Spaulding. Most of the time, that's exactly what the customer ended up doing. Thus, Grand Spaulding made the sale, and in order for the vehicle to continue to run its best, it was recommended that it be serviced at Grand Spaulding. The Kraus brothers took a risk by ordering so many high-performance models, hoping that the enthusiasts would want

Plush to the max, the latest Grand Spaulding 1968 GSS Dodge Dart is tailored to cosset its occupants in leather and rich carpet. Yet with a huge tachometer in the driver's face and a beefy Hurst shifter at hand, it isn't hard to bury passengers deep into the seat foam.

more than a grocery-getter. The risk paid off with Grand Spaulding becoming Mopar Mecca.

Another way to please the customer was to "recommend" some performance-enhancing components, such as headers, rear axle gear sets, and such, which could be easily financed and installed right at the dealership. The financed price of the vehicle

would include all of the performance parts: One-stop shopping.

In 1963, Grand Spaulding Dodge sold performance cars but didn't race. In fact, Norm and Lenny Kraus didn't know the first thing about drag racing. That changed the day a former customer who had bought one of the Max Wedge cars walked into the dealership and approached Norm Kraus with a proposal. If Grand Spaulding would supply him with a set of spark plugs and a pair of seat belts, he'd put the dealership's name on the side of his car. Kraus figured, what the hell, and gave him the parts. That weekend, the car was raced at the Chicago Amphitheater, a huge building that hosted everything from concerts to rodeos. The feature that weekend was

Some things never change, thank heaven. The rear of the new Dart Hemi is the perfect place to position the dealer emblem, as virtually every other driver will get a good look at the tail. It helps when there is 825 horsepower under the hood.

Here is Gary Dyer posing with another in a long line of Grand Spaulding Dodge drag cars in front of the dealership's small showroom. Dyer told Mr. Norm that racing in classes inhabited by customers was counter to selling performance cars. Thus the dealership fought in the upper race classes, building goodwill and getting heavy exposure. *Gary Dyer Collection*

By purchasing a competitive car and fitting it with a new engine, Grand Spaulding Dodge and Gary Dyer quickly started gathering wins. Dyer would be Mr. Norm's chief driver well into the 1970s. *Gary Dyer Collection*

indoor drag racing. Come the following Monday, the phone started ringing off the hook. People would say, Hey, that car you sponsored won its race. Grand Spaulding sold three cars on Monday to people who saw the name on the side of the race car. Again, performance put money into Grand Spaulding's pocket.

The higher profile that drag racing gave Grand Spaulding Dodge worked well with the new "Mr. Norm's Sport Club," a dealer-sponsored organization that allowed its members to save money on performance parts and service, as well as purchase new vehicles for just $200 over invoice. A newsletter was sent to members notifying them of the latest and greatest at the dealership. One of the primary reasons for Grand Spaulding Dodge's success throughout the 1960s was its three-pronged approach to the performance market. The most visible effort was the selling of high-performance vehicles. Racing helped get Grand Spaulding Dodge's name in front of the hard-core racing fan, but customers walked

onto the showroom floor looking for a street car that could kick butt on Saturday night.

The two other areas that Mr. Norm worked hard on were the parts department and the service department. It wasn't unusual to walk to the parts counter and pass a half dozen Hemi engines on stands. Grand Spaulding Dodge advertised that they had Hemis in stock, so come on over and let us install one in your car! Of the six Hemi engines on display, only one was ready for sale; the others were old race engines that had broken. They would get an exterior freshening, so that they looked factory-fresh. But often they lacked internal components such as a crankshaft, pistons, or connecting rods. If more than one Hemi engine was needed for a customer, a quick phone call to Detroit would see crated elephants on the next truck to Chicago.

Last but by no means least was the service department. Grand Spaulding Dodge's reputation depended on solid, strong muscle cars rolling across the curb, and with a Clayton Chassis Dynamometer, it was

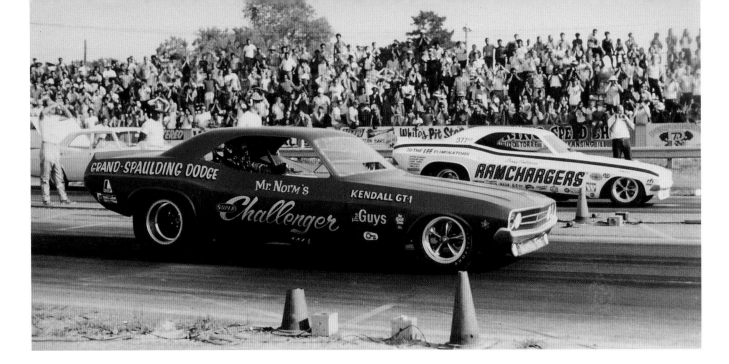

Inching up to the starting line, Gary Dyer prepares to take on the Ramchargers Hemi Funny Car. Unlike today's race cars that have sponsor decals covering every square inch of bodywork, the race cars in the early 1970s actually had some open paint. *Gary Dyer Collection*

possible to set up an engine in near race conditions. He called it a "power tune," and it consisted of rejetting the carburetor and recurving the distributor. Mr. Norm quickly gained a reputation for selling the hottest Dodges, period.

In 1963, the inaugural SEMA show hit the bleachers under Dodger Stadium, and Norm Kraus attended, taking back to the dealership a determination to expand his parts department into a national force. He succeeded, making Grand Spaulding Dodge *the* top source for performance Mopar parts.

Grand Spaulding Dodge formed a racing team in 1964, made up of two cars, a Max Wedge and a Hemi Ram. The team was run by the same group that later campaigned the Chi-Town Hustler, but the results weren't what Kraus wanted. Toward the end of the season, he met Gary Dyer, and together they hatched a plan to put the Grand Spaulding Dodge name in front of drag-racing fans without alienating buyers. It didn't make any sense to compete in the same drag classes that Grand Spaulding Dodge's customers competed in. The dealership had the advantage with the latest equipment and a larger budget, and as Gary Dyer recalls, "these kids are coming in and getting their cars dyno'ed, and we're running better stuff than them. Maybe we should get out of that class,

have a car that's a symbol of the dealership. We should run a blown car; then we wouldn't compete with the kids."

When the 1965 drag-racing season opened, Grand Spaulding Dodge had a new car. It was a post car that had the rear wheels kicked forward 15 inches. The car ran on gasoline for a bit, then it was shifted to nitro. In mid-1965 they bought the former "Color Me Gone" factory-altered wheelbase acid-dipped Dodge Coronet of Roger Lindamood. The supercharged engine was pulled from the post car and installed in the Coronet. The Color Me Gone lettering was removed and "Grand Spaulding Dodge" was applied. Unchanged was the body color. This supercharged Hemi caught the racing world by surprise when it covered Lion's Dragway in just 8.63 seconds against Don Gay's GTO, making drag-racing history and spreading the name of Grand Spaulding Dodge from coast to coast.

Seeing the trend for muscle cars growing at a rapid clip, Kraus asked the factory for an entry-level performance car, something that could compete with the Chevrolet Nova. Dodge sent Grand Spaulding a 1967 Dart with a 273-cubic-inch V-8. Kraus called and asked where the 383 engine was and was told that the engine wouldn't fit under the Dart's hood. Kraus told his parts manager to take the small-block out and see what it

With an undulating shoulder line and a tapering nose, the 1971 Super Bee was a rolling Coke bottle. The full-width grill emphasized the massive width of the car, necessitated by the need for any engine, including the huge Hemi, to fit comfortably under the hood. *Mike Mueller*

Any enthusiast, regardless of their preference, has to admit that the 426 Hemi was an impressive-looking engine. Race-bred, it was happiest running at high RPMs, it didn't much care for cold weather, and it tended to burn oil. Yet it was the source of considerable adoration. *Mike Mueller*

would take to install the big-block. The next morning, Kraus was told that the car was ready. By moving the motor mounts a little, notching the K-member, and installing a heat shield to protect the steering box, the car was on the road. The resulting potent package was shown to Dodge executives and engineers, who saw a low-cost street bruiser. The factory released it as a Dart 383 GTS. While the engine was a tight fit, especially in the exhaust manifold department, it didn't deter Mr. Norm. Next up; if a 383 will fit, let's see if a 440 will too. Norm Kraus called in a favor from the factory and had a run of 50 1968 Dodge Darts fitted with the potent 440-cubic-inch engine and durable 727 Torqueflite automatic transmission. Grand Spaulding plucked the letter "T" from the GTS emblems and inserted another "S," creating the GSS 440 Dart. It fit, though it was no roomier in the engine compartment. To extract real horsepower, headers were needed to let the big-block breathe, and that required some cutting away of the inner front fenders. While not the most elegant solution, it worked, and GSS 440 Darts were kicking butt on the street.

Grand Spaulding fed the need for Mopar performance through the 1960s, becoming the No. 1 Dodge dealer in the world in 1974. Not every car that rolled out of Grand Spaulding was a muscle car; lots of

In the latter half of the classic muscle car era, Chrysler signed on with Warner Brothers studio to use the Road Runner art on some of its vehicles. Taking it another step, Chrysler used a slew of cartoon-like graphics to market their cars, such as the 1971 Super Bee, a take-off on the car being a B-body platform. *Mike Mueller*

"normal" vehicles were sold as well. And don't overlook the used-car market; the Kraus brothers sure didn't. They loved having scores of used muscle cars on the lot, many of them non-Dodges. Converts to the Mopar faith they were called.

In the early 1970s, it was becoming clear that the performance market was going to go away as increasingly tough federal rules regarding emissions dovetailed with rising insurance rates to doom the traditional muscle car. Most performance dealers folded up their tents and became shadows of their former selves. Grand Spaulding, on the other hand, took a look at the auto biz and saw that the next big thing was in van conversions.

In the summers starting in 1970, the van conversion outfits would be calling all of the dealers trying to get vans to bring to their facilities to convert into rolling living rooms. They would have a difficult time coming up with enough vans, as the factories would be shut down to get ready for the next model year. In the spring of 1973, Norm Kraus called up Bob

Evoking the famous Ramchargers name, the Super Bee's hood scoop would rise to ingest fresh air into the engine compartment, as well as dazzle the vehicle occupants and bystanders. Engine callouts on the hood left no doubt that the big guy had arrived. *Mike Mueller*

Long, low, and wide, the Super Bee was a full-size car with a huge engine and a smallish interior. But it made a hell of a statement on the road. The contrasting vinyl roof and full-length body stripes made for a visually arresting package, while the Hemi under the hood could just get you arrested. *Mike Mueller*

McCurry, head of Dodge, and told him that he wanted to order another 1,000 vans. McCurry asked why he needed so many vans. Kraus told him. The order went through; the vans were built and delivered. Shortly after that, the phones started ringing, as the van conversion companies were looking for vehicles again. Grand Spaulding was the only dealer that had the vans. Ka-ching.

Another avenue of income that Grand Spaulding Dodge pursued was fleet sales. Kraus hired a full-time fleet manager to aggressively market fleet sales to police, government agencies, and rental car companies. So widespread was Grand Spaulding's leasing, it was able to supply the entire Chicago Police Department with its cruisers. Many of these Mr. Norm cars can be seen in the movie *The Blues Brothers*.

Grand Spaulding Dodge closed its doors in 1975, and Norm Kraus retired in 1977, having led Grand Spaulding Dodge to dizzying heights. Yet Kraus isn't finished with high performance. He has developed and is selling a "new" 1968 Dart, this time packing a 735-horsepower Hemi. It will run 10-second quarter-mile runs, and still travel to the grocery store (as long as you don't mind setting off every car alarm in the lot). Kraus has come a long way from selling cars at his father's gas station.

# CHAPTER 7

# FRED GIBB CHEVROLET

## *SMALL TOWN, BIG CAR*

Sitting on State Road 9 in central Illinois about 15 miles from the Mississippi River is the tiny farming town of La Harpe. Fewer than 1,500 people call it home, and in post-war America, virtually every small town had a Chevrolet dealer. In 1948, Fred Gibb Jr. opened his Chevrolet dealership on the west side of town, selling a lot of sedans and pickups. Yet over time, he would become known to the drag-racing community as the father of one of the most potent automobiles to ever roll out of Detroit.

Pulling cool air from the base of the windshield, the ZL-1 Camaro had a voracious appetite for combustible material. This was your basic race car that you could drive on the street.

Rare, subtle, and stupid-fast, the 1969 Camaro ZL-1 used an all-aluminum 427-cubic-inch race engine to pound humility into everyone else. Only one Camaro ZL-1 was built with a vinyl roof from the factory.

COPO 9560AA was corporate-speak for a 1969 ZL-1 Camaro. With open headers, the engine would dyno at 575 horsepower, yet its rated output of 430 was tacit acknowledgment that the insurance companies were starting to exert pressure on Detroit.

From almost any angle, a ZL-1 Camaro was a visually underwhelming machine. There were very few external markings to hint at the thermonuclear device under the hood.

Fred Gibb sold Chevroletsand was happy to stick with that. The dealership employed about a dozen people. Gibb erected a new building in 1961, a single-level structure, not fancy, but a clean design. Also in 1961, he hired a young man in his 20s, Herb Fox, to work on the showroom floor as a salesman. Fox had been a drag-racing enthusiast for years before he started working at Gibb Chevrolet; at the time of hiring he was racing a D/Gasser.

Gibb didn't care for drag racing, thinking that it attracted the wrong kind of crowd. Fox remembers that "Fred was kind of a religious man, and he didn't go for childish, foolish things like I was interested in. He wasn't into it; he said it cost a lot of money." Yet Fox was Gibb Chevrolet's best salesman; in 1965, Fox sold 368 cars out of the small dealership. One day in 1966 Fox was about to head out for another weekend of racing at the local drag strip in Cahokia when Gibb approached him and asked what he was doing. Fox remembers, "I told him I was going racing. He asked if he could come along. I figured it would probably be my job. I said okay, if you want to go, get in. We came back and he'd changed his mind about racing."

The extra cost of a ZL-1 was evidenced under the hood, not in the interior. Bone stock, the ZL-1 driver sat in an environment identical to what the owner of a six-cylinder Camaro would enjoy. The difference became crystal clear the moment the engine was fired. One sounded like it was ready for a trip to the grocery store, the other sounded like it was in the staging lanes.

The breakdown on ZL-1 Camaro production was as follows: 47 were built with four-speed manual transmissions, and 22 were equipped with three-speed automatics.

Bigger numbers were always better than smaller numbers, and in 1969, few engines packed more punch than Chevrolet's 427. When you add an aluminum block and a ton of other race parts, the number took on new significance.

Chevrolet introduced the Camaro for 1967, and Gibb ordered a Z/28 to use as a demonstrator. After it had driven potential customers around for a month, Gibb approached Fox and said, "You want to go in on a race car?" Fox said that he didn't want to spend all that money. He said he remembers Gibb telling him, "That's okay, I'll just take the demo and make a race car out of it and you can drive it."

But there was a hitch, as Fox recalls. "He wanted to run it stock, and you can't win running stock. Well, it was May or June, and I'd gone down to St. Louis to see a Cardinals game. Somehow I got lost in East St. Louis. Dick Harrell was building 427 Camaros in an old gas station; I pulled in there asking directions how to get back across the river. He said, 'What do you do?' I told him, 'I sell cars at Fred Gibb Chevrolet. Are these cars for sale?' 'Yes,' said Harrell, 'I've got a red one and a black one. They have 427s with dual quads.' I told him I'd talk to my boss. When I got back to La Harpe, I told Fred about them, and he said to 'get in the car, we're going to St. Louis.' We went

Top Gibb salesman and drag car driver Herb Fox is suited up and ready to run the quarter-mile. Safety equipment requirements in the 1960s were far less stringent than today. *Helen Gibb Collection*

Note the luxurious working conditions that the Fred Gibb racing team enjoyed between runs. With Dick Harrell behind the wheel, the odds were rather good that the team was taking home a trophy on Sunday. *Helen Gibb Collection*

down there and bought both of them." Harrell started working with Gibb improving their Z/28, and when the season had ended, the Royal Plum Camaro, called "Little Hoss," earned 35 wins in 1967—and no losses.

The following year Little Hoss was at it again, racking up an impressive 30 wins to only three losses. That performance earned Fox the AHRA World Championship Stocker trophy in 1968, and that level of winning got Fred Gibb thinking that he would like to achieve even more victories. Another driver added to the Gibb roster in 1968 was none other than famed drag racer Dick Harrell.

Gibb was friends with Vince Piggins, the engineering chief that led Chevrolet to develop many high-performance parts and packages. The two had met in South Dakota in 1966 while pheasant hunting, and they hit it off. Gibb wanted to compete in NHRA events, and he had an idea for an engine/transmission combination. With a lightweight body, such as a Chevy II, the installation of Chevrolet's big-block engine could produce an interesting vehicle. Bolting an automatic transmission allowed the car to run in Super Stock/C and SS/CA classes. The only problem was the Chevy II didn't come with a big-block/automatic package in 1968. Gibb wasn't going to let that deter him; he called his friend Vince, up in Detroit.

Unknown to the public was a way for dealers to order vehicles in bulk for fleet sales, the Central Office Production Order, or COPO. This system existed to allow vehicles with special needs such as taxis, police cars, and governmental cars to be ordered without the dealer jumping through too many hoops. Like any Chevrolet dealer, he was aware of the COPO procedure. But he thought that he might be able to use it to his advantage. The National Hot Rod Association required a minimum of 50 cars built to qualify it for racing. Piggins had assured Gibb that with a production run of at least 50 units, it would be possible to run some special-request cars down the production line. Gibb opened his order book and filled out the paperwork, requesting a batch of COPO #9738 Chevy II Novas.

Equipped with an L78, solid-lifter, 375-horsepower, 396-cubic-inch engine, each was bolted to a Turbo Hydramatic 400 three-speed automatic transmission. By July 15, 1968, all 50 cars had been built and delivered to La Harpe. Fox remembers that Gibb Chevrolet sold all of his COPO Novas at full sticker without a single trade-in.

But this is where things got interesting. Approximately 20 of the Novas were sent down to Dick Harrell's shop in Kansas City, Missouri, where the 396 was ejected from the engine compartment and replaced with a 427-cubic-inch powerplant. Harrell had observed while working for Don

Dick Harrell relaxes with the Gibb race car in the staging lanes. Most race cars didn't have such an elaborate paint job, but Harrell was a big name, and the eye-catching finish put the Fred Gibb name in front of potential customers. *Helen Gibb Collection*

Yenko that a nationwide distribution system was key to success when selling very high performance vehicles. He entered into agreements with about a dozen Chevrolet dealerships across the country to sell his modified vehicles. Thus after they had been massaged at Harrell's shop, they were transported to waiting dealers.

The success in selling the COPO Novas led Gibb and Harrell to try a small run of high-performance Camaros in 1969. Once again, Vince Piggins was approached, and plans were laid to build another run of 50 cars, this time equipped with a 427-cubic-inch engine. But not just any 427; the engine in mind was the new ZL-1. With its aluminum block, heads, and intake manifold, the big-block weighed only 500 pounds, about the same as the common 327-cubic-inch engine. However, it developed power unlike any factory small-block. Built to compete in the Can-Am series, the ZL-1s installed in the Camaros were your basic de-turned race engine. It developed well over 500 horsepower, and with more than 450 lb-ft of torque, there wasn't a street tire that could survive a heavy right foot. Harrell and Gibb thought they had a winner.

Gibb placed the order for COPO #9560 and waited. He had been told by Chevrolet that this street-legal race car would cost about $4,900 each. Gibb felt that enough racers would pony up that amount of money to make the order worthwhile. The first two cars arrived at the La Harpe dealership on December 31, 1968, in minus-22-degree weather. Gibb had to use a tow truck to pull the cars off the trailer because they refused to start.

When the first bill for the cars showed up on his desk, it showed that Gibb owed $7,269 for each car. Fox

Fred Gibb's first experiment with the COPO system resulted in 50 Novas being built with healthy 396-cubic-inch engines. Herb Fox remembers that they sold well, encouraging Gibb to think about ordering another COPO performance car. *Helen Gibb Collection*

Dick Harrell did engine swaps at his shop, then sold the results through a select dealer network, including Fred Gibb Chevrolet. *Helen Gibb Collection*

remembers that Gibb "about had a heart attack. That was as much as a Cadillac." After Gibb's heart started again, he called Chevrolet and asked about the hefty price increase over the original estimate. Chevy responded with the news that starting in 1969, the word had come down from on high that research and development costs associated with limited-run vehicles would be borne by the customer. In this case, that would be Fred Gibb Chevrolet.

Quickly contacting Chevrolet, Gibb explained that the huge price jump was going to make it impossible for him to buy all 50 ZL-1 Camaros. Chevrolet, in an unprecedented move, agreed to buy back the bulk of the cars. Fox remembered, "We got 13 sold, but we didn't know what we were going to do with the rest of them. We pulled into Detroit for the drags, and Gibb got called up to the tower. When he came down from the tower I asked him what happened. He said that the general manager there thought it [the ZL-1] was the hot deal and wanted one. I told him to come to La Harpe and take them. He came with a semi and took all but one. We had it two years before we ever got rid of it." The rest of the initial order for 50 cars went to other dealers around the country. By the time 1969 ZL-1 Camaro production ended, 69 of the monsters were built.

Back at the La Harpe dealership, ZL-1 #1, a Dusk Blue, automatic-transmission-equipped car, was shipped to Dick Harrell's shop in Missouri, where in three weeks' time it was race-prepared and painted Harrell's color, candy apple red. Herb Fox drove it in its inaugural outing, beating Ronnie Sox. During the rest of the 1969 racing season, it traversed the country, posting a best time of 10.05 seconds at 139 mph. Fox handled most of the driving duties, yet he was underwhelmed with the ZL-1 engine. "That ZL-1 never would run. The cylinder sleeves

Looking very dapper, Fred Gibb stands by his Nova race car on a beautiful Illinois afternoon. This is the vehicle that Dick Harrell campaigned. *Helen Gibb Collection*

always popped out. We put an engine on the dyno and it blew up right there. We brought it home and put a Diamond Racing steel motor in. We had problems with the car in the first part of the season, but when we got driver Jim Hayter, he really made it fly. He got that car into the 9.80s. That was pretty fast back then."

The dealership was enjoying national recognition, and while that was prized by any dealer, coming from a town with 1,000 people made it especially sweet. The service department was staying busy, not only with regular street cars, but performance work as well. The service manager at the dealership, Ben Wright, who had built a Pro Stocker with Fox, had about seven young mechanics working in the service department, and they were enthused about turning wrenches on the performance machinery. Fox recalls, "We put a 427 in just about anything you'd drag in

there." Visiting race teams would often stop at Gibb Chevrolet and work on the race cars in the service area. Often, mechanics would be spinning wrenches all night, followed by a trial run of the race engine. Fox remembers that "you couldn't hear yourself half the time for the engines." The residents of La Harpe were not amused.

Fox remembers the parts department well. "We were the king for 500 miles around us. We'd buy 50 four-speeds at a time, we'd buy 50 427s at a time; if Chevrolet made it, we had it. On a Saturday, it was like a circus around here. They'd come from everywhere. The parts department was run by Bill Brabill. He was just a farmer that Fred hired one day to be the parts man. Bib overalls, you would have thought he wouldn't know the back of the car from the front, but he knew those parts backwards and forwards. We were kind of a low-scale deal at one time. "

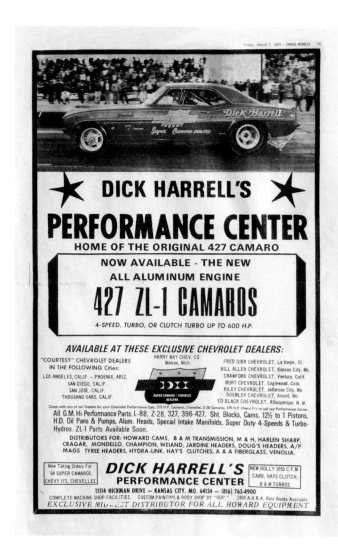

When Fred Gibb ordered 50 ZL-1 Camaros, he thought he was paying a far lower price than the final bill came to. Many of the cars were returned, some of them ending up in Dick Harrell's hands. *Helen Gibb Collection*

papers. I didn't really need to be a salesman; the car sold itself." Fox would handle all of the transaction, himself. Unlike bigger dealerships, there was no sales manager, no F&I department. The salesman would be involved with the sales process from the customer walking in the door to the car rolling over the curb.

Gibb believed that having a wide range of cars in stock would prevent buyers from going over to the next little town's Chevy dealer. Sitting on the Route 9 lot would be a broad selection of cars, such as the COPO Novas, ZL-1 Camaros, and Corvettes. In a small town, you could only sell so many vehicles to the local inhabitants. So the vast bulk of Gibb Chevrolet's business was from outside the La Harpe area.

In 1970, Fred Gibb Chevrolet sponsored Dick Harrell as he drove a new '70 Camaro Funny Car, but it was a nitro-burning, 200-mph monster that had virtually no connection with a street Camaro. Then in 1971, the 1969 car was pulled out and raced, with Jim Hayter campaigning the car. It was brutally fast, covering the quarter-mile during the AHRA World Points Finals on October 8, 1971, in just 9.63 seconds at a blistering 143 mph, winning the Pro Stock World Championship. This was to be the high point for the Gibb Racing Team. At the close of the season, Gibb decided to step away from racing. The performance automotive landscape had changed, and not for the better. The cars coming out of the factories were down on power, emission regulations were poised to further emasculate the muscle car, and the insurance companies had lowered the boom. Fred Gibb Chevrolet went back to selling bread-and-butter vehicles.

Gibb sold the dealership in 1984 and retired, and today the building is a tire shop. The boom times lasted less than five years, yet this tiny dealership in a small Midwestern town had an impact that was felt from coast to coast. Fred Gibb Chevrolet was proof that enthusiasm and drive will take you farther than cubic dollars.

Buyers would come into the dealership looking for automotive trouble and would be directed to Fox. He handled the sale of the high-performance vehicles, whether it was a Camaro, Chevelle, Corvette, or any other Chevrolet product. Fox laughed. "First they wanted to go for a ride in my demo. How that poor little thing took it I don't know. I had a 4:10 gear; that's like having two motors in a car. I'd hit the gas and their eyes would get real wide, they couldn't believe it. I'd take them down the highway, down Route 9. We had a deal, maybe not real fair, but back in those days we'd hook up the financing, we could put a guy in any car for $50 a month. It had a balloon payment on the end. Then they outlawed that, so we went to 10-year financing. Most of the buyers were young people like me; they couldn't wait to sign the

# CHAPTER 8

# BERGER CHEVROLET

## *MULTIGENERATIONAL PERFORMANCE*

Grand Rapids, Michigan, is not normally the first city that springs to your mind when performance enthusiasts mention the home of some of the most significant muscle dealers. A couple of hours' drive away from Detroit, it's the birthplace of President Gerald Ford, and the lake-effect snow is a pain in the butt. Yet it's one of the few dealerships still in business from the glory days when an 18-year-old could walk onto a dealer's lot and drive off in a rolling hand grenade with the pin pulled. Actually, Berger Chevrolet will sell you one of those today.

While most performance dealers used decals or tape graphics to denote the dealership name, Berger went the extra mile to have special cast-metal emblems made. Besides giving the vehicle a touch of class, the emblems were permanent. *Mike Mueller*

Looking like it just rolled off of a race track, a 1970 Berger Camaro was all fins, spoilers, and bulging sheet metal. The tall hood was a modification of the L88 Corvette hood from 1968. *Mike Mueller*

When a vehicle is moving, the base of the windshield builds up pressure. Automotive engineers often use this area of high pressure as a source of engine induction air. Berger was no exception, as the rear of the huge hood opened to the rear, allowing air to flow into the carburetor. *Mike Mueller*

Berger Chevrolet was founded in 1925 by William H. Berger. From day one, Chevrolet was the name on the sign. Located in a former blacksmith shop, it sold the full line of Bow Tie products. The parts and service departments ran just like any other facility, and business was steady. William's son Dale started working at the dealership in 1932, and in turn, Dale Jr. came on board. He had attended General Motors Institute, graduating in 1958, and then went to work at the family dealership in the parts department.

In 1964, Dale Jr. became the general manager, and he was interested not only in furthering the family business, but also in profiting from the burgeoning performance scene. As a successful Chevrolet dealer, Dale had his ear tuned for future trends, and he saw that the increase in factory horsepower and the rise of an entire generation of

Shaped in a wind tunnel, the huge rear spoiler generated usable downforce. From the rear, the second-generation Camaro's European styling influences are evident. *Mike Mueller*

Dale Berger thought of "Prescribed Power" as a catch phrase that covered the dealership's performance-oriented products. The emblem is intended to resemble a pharmacist's mortar and pestle. *Mike Mueller*

enthusiasts meant that the demand for go-fast parts was only going to grow. His business plan was to use a performance parts business to bring customers into the facility, and if he sold some of them vehicles as well . . .

Berger Chevrolet opened a new building in 1965 on 28th Street, surrounded by shopping malls. The following year, Berger felt that the time was ripe for entering the performance market, and the first step was to hire Jim O'Connor. At that time O'Connor was writing service at a Grand Rapids Pontiac dealership, but before that, he had been the performance parts manager at Nickey Chevrolet in Chicago. Nickey had a huge parts department built in its former body shop, and O'Connor had been tapped to lead it. In his spare time, he raced a Corvette, so he knew the performance terrain. He brought that knowledge with him to Grand Rapids.

But O'Connor didn't stay at the dealership long. He was replaced by Bob Delamar, and sales continued

to increase. Berger had a large, conventional parts department, with a parts manager, wholesale parts people, parts runners, and even a parts representative that went around to body shops. The performance parts department only had one man who catered to high performance. Customers walking up to the parts department would see two counters, side by side. One counter handled regular parts transactions, while the other counter was used for the performance business.

It got to the point that on November 25, 1968, Delamar asked 21-year-old Jim Luikens, who had been hanging around the performance parts counter for a

Jim Luikens went through up to four El Caminos a year, picking up and delivering parts at Berger Chevrolet. At a dealership where the parts department was one of the largest in the country, there was little downtime for the employees behind the counter. *Jim Luikens Collection*

Berger Chevrolet's crack performance salesman, Mike Wawee, was an active drag racer. This involvement in racing helped Wawee understand what was needed on the track to win. He was able to direct his customers to the best package for their budget and needs. *Jim Luikens Collection*

while getting parts for his drag car, a 1957 Pontiac wagon that competed in G/Stock Auto, if he would like a job behind the counter. Luikens recalls, "I'd be talking to Bob, half bench racing, half strategy, half look-up stuff. He had grown the department where he really needed some help." Luikens was working at Kroger at the time. "I decided to take a 25 percent pay cut and follow my heart. I was a hard-core car guy."

It wasn't long before Berger Chevrolet's parts department was *the* source of performance parts in western Michigan. Jim Luikens remembers that in the late 1960s, "Berger was a pretty hard-core place when it came to parts. Even though they didn't stock Pontiac stuff, if you needed something, they knew where to get it. If you were a serious racer, and you needed the hard-core stuff, they could get it."

Luikens was the right man at the right place at the right time. He quickly found out that he was fluent reading parts manuals. "Numbers come easy to me, long strings of numbers. I took to the numbering system quite

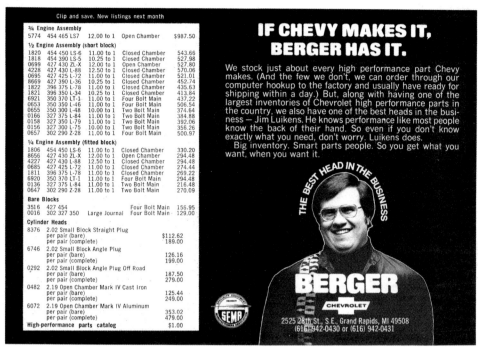

What you're looking at is a computer. Jim Luikens modestly acknowledged his skill with numbers; performance enthusiasts called it a gift. Having cracked the codes in the parts manuals, he was able to piece together the ideal combination of parts needed for almost any application. *Jim Luikens Collection*

This was the right man at the right place at the right time. If Berger Chevrolet didn't have the part in stock, Jim Luikens knew where he could lay his hands on one, pronto. *Jim Luikens Collection*

naturally." With the plentiful street action, the drivers swarmed into the dealership to replace broken components, upgrade equipment, and learn about the latest and greatest. Yet, as Luikens points out, "You have to remember, Chevrolet was making a strong statement; they weren't in racing. So they had to hide these things in plain sight. General Motors applied a methodology and a terminology that was for the most part consistent. By studying the parts book, and applying some educated guesses, I got pretty good at speaking their unspoken language."

Delamar and Luikens quickly developed a working rhythm, with Delamar working the phones and Luikens pulling and packing the parts. Luikens laughs when he thinks about those days. "I'd work behind the counter all day, then take a dinner break when we closed the shop at 6. I'd get a bite to eat, then go back and pack the orders we'd taken. I usually wouldn't get out of there before 10:30. In those days, UPS didn't have the rights to deliver in all 50 states. So we shipped whatever we could by UPS. I remember two states, North Carolina and New York, two of our top states for volume, didn't have UPS delivery. If someone in North Carolina ordered a camshaft, I had to take it to the post office and stand in line with everyone else. We'd ship it out by parcel post. Finally UPS got permission to ship to all 50 states, and that was a big day because we didn't have to go to the post office anymore."

In June 1970, Bob Delamar left Berger Chevrolet to start his own speed shop in Grand Rapids. Luikens was promoted to be the high-performance parts manager, and his laid-back, every-man approach to treating customers allowed him to get along with everyone by treating everybody the same. "If they came in, they had a need, and I really tried to solve their problem and fill their need. That was the thing that I lived by."

It's the mid-1960s, and the sun's always shining above Berger Chevrolet in Grand Rapids, Michigan. The modern dealership boasted an all-glass showroom and an impressive display of quality used cars next to the curb. *Jim Luikens Collection*

Luikens' ability both with the parts books and with the customers resulted in massive sales. According to Luikens, "Dale Berger's philosophy was to sell the parts. We'd sell lots of performance cars, we even did a few engine swaps, and by a few, I mean about half a dozen a year with an upgraded engine conversion through the service department. Dale was never very interested pursuing that; he dabbled in it certainly. But he really pursued the parts, because I assume he felt that for every guy that could afford a new car, there were thousands of guys that needed a camshaft for the cars they already had. He decided to sell the thousands of camshafts rather than the one car.

"Nobody pursued the parts sales like Berger. We ordered crate engines and short blocks every week.

We've have anywhere around 20 sitting in the parts department at any time."

Berger agreed. "That's exactly right. We really pushed the parts. We went out to SEMA and bought a lot of aftermarket stuff, but the core of the parts business that really brought people in was the General Motors parts, the cylinder heads, the bare blocks, the camshafts. We sent containers of parts to South Africa, to Australia. We had one guy drive all the way from Salt Lake City to pick up an engine. We did a very good business; the high-performance parts alone generated about $40–$45 thousand a month."

In a form of industrial cloak and dagger, Berger remembers that "We had a pretty good source within General Motors that kept us abreast of when new cylinder heads were coming out, [plus other] engine modifications."

In late 1966, the Camaro rolled into showrooms, and *finally*, Chevrolet had a car to battle the Ford Mustang. But Berger recalls that when the Camaro came out, "It didn't sell well, not nearly as well as they thought it would. Chevrolet was eager to do anything, so we put a package together; we called them Grand Rapids Camaros. We had some emblems made for the front fenders, and we used Grand Prix lettering, GR, to put on

The prices for high-performance engines and components seem very reasonable today, but these were serious prices in the late 1960s and early '70s. Still, one can dream. *Jim Luikens Collection*

It's the early 1970s, and you're standing at the high-performance parts counter at Berger Chevrolet. Besides every Chevrolet factory performance part you could think of close at hand, the dealership also handled popular aftermarket components, such as Doug's Headers, Hurst shifters, and Mallory ignition systems. Check out that intake manifold on the peg board. *Jim Luikens Collection*

the vinyl roof. They put the emblems on the cars at the Norwood, Ohio, plant. We sold about 35 of those things in a month, and that really got General Motors excited to see that local dealers could do something and the car could be sold. It was a very salable car; it just needed exposure and advertising. Once we did that, we had a kind of a sweet spot in our heart for the Camaro, which to this day we have."

In an effort to capitalize on the skill of Luikens, Berger Chevrolet's advertising agency, Johnson & Dean, got together with Berger with the idea of showing

Luikens in a series of print ads that would tout the high-performance parts manager's skill behind the counter. Berger said he felt that "if we've got the guy that's got the knowledge, why not advertise him?" These advertisements put a face with the ad copy, calling Luikens "The Best Head in the Business." Berger remembers that "We had a girl in some ads. She was out of the Playboy modeling agency in Chicago. She was used in some of the ads and in the catalog pictures. She ended up in New York working on soap operas." Another marketing idea that Berger came up with was a slogan

The check-in desk is busy at the 1968 National Corvette meet at Berger Chevrolet in Grand Rapids, Michigan. Who came in the Mustang? *Berger Collection*

"Prescribed Power." A local decal shop was approached and a pharmaceutical "mortar and pestle" were incorporated into the logo. It was affixed to various parts of the performance cars and visually set Berger's hot cars apart from the rest of the herd.

One of the salesmen at Berger, Mike Wawee, was the go-to guy when customers would come in looking for a performance car. The other salesmen would direct the buyer to Wawee, who would sit down with the customer and determine just what they wanted.

A significant point about Berger was the sale of factory-assembled high-performance cars, as opposed to dealer-assembled cars. The latter method to performance wasn't a path that was heavily traveled. Berger recalls that "the COPO system worked well, if a dealer knew about it. If I had allocation, they had to ship it to me. We had another mole in Chevrolet, and we found out about the COPO from him. We got allocation from the zone, so we had the availability to order the cars. A small dealer that might sell five or six Camaros in a year would have a problem, but we were selling about thirty a month, so we had plenty of allocation. When we ordered the COPO cars, we ordered them in two different batches. The zone took good care of us, making sure we had the allocation. Mike Wawee was very good at setting us up with the moles. The informant would come to town, and Mike and he would go out for a couple of drinks, or go to the drag races. We'd get the latest news about what was coming out, especially the COPOs. He'd say here's the latest COPO number, here's what it contains, and here's how you have to order it. I'd call the zone and make sure I had allocation and I would get the car."

Luikens remembers his good friend Wawee. "He was the one that really put Berger on the map when it

This Corvette convertible was only a year old, and the owner had already pulled the bumpers, probably to improve the car's chances on a race circuit. Gotta love the fashions of the day. *Berger Collection*

Dale Berger understood the worth of "Racing on Sunday, selling on Monday." To that end, he sponsored a number of drag strip racers, including Dick Arons' 1969 Camaro, competing in Super Stock/E Class. *Jim Luikens Collection*

came to selling high-performance vehicles off the showroom floor. He would order large batches of cars, months ahead of when we'd need them. He'd somehow know how to equip them. We'd get so many Camaros with big blocks, some with automatics, so many with sticks, or they'd have small blocks. He would order all of the cars for Berger, not just the performance cars."

Berger remembers Wawee well. "You'd come in to buy a performance car, and you'd sit down with Mike. He'd charm you; he was very good. He really knew high performance. We had a pretty selection of product. We'd have 10–15 Z/28s, maybe 10–15 SS 396 Chevelles, hot Novas, and Camaros. He and I even did a book for Ford Motor Company about selling high-performance cars. They wined and dined me out at Riverside Raceway; then I found out why. But they were good people."

Berger Chevrolet's service department employed some of mechanics who just worked on performance cars. Berger recalled, "We had a couple of guys that were really good, especially Chuck Honeycutt. He did some racing himself, and was very good at installing the stuff. We didn't do a huge amount of engine conversions, and none when the emission stuff came out. You could get yourself in trouble. That was when things started to really slow down."

Exacerbating the downward spiral of performance, President Nixon instituted a price and wage freeze in 1972. It was lifted in 1974, and suddenly the cost of parts went through the roof. Needless to say, sales plummeted. In concert with the rise in prices was the Gas Crisis in October 1973. The demand for performance cars and parts dried up overnight. In 1974, Berger Chevrolet sold more than 400 Vegas.

For the next couple of decades, Berger Chevrolet sold mainline Chevrolet products. But in 1999, Dale Berger's son Matt Berger, who had stepped into his father's role at the dealership, was approached by Matt Murphy of GMMG about building a Camaro with a genuine increase in performance. Murphy pointed out that a following was in place that remembered the performance days at Berger. By using the prowess of Chevrolet Engineering and careful suspension upgrades, the resulting vehicles were modern iterations of the monsters that dealerships sold many years ago. Using the established dealer network, GMMG built scores of Camaros that offered neck-snapping performance in a street-legal package. Berger led the resurgence, and today, with the next generation Camaro on the near horizon, Berger is poised to tap into the enthusiasm. With four generations of Bergers associated with Chevrolet, it shouldn't surprise anyone if more tire smoke is seen trailing a Berger Chevy.

# CHAPTER 9

# YENKO CHEVROLET

## *WELCOME TO CANONSBURG, HOME OF PERRY COMO AND DON YENKO*

In 1960s America, the term "performance car" usually denoted a vehicle that could cover the quarter-mile as quickly as possible. Handling curves and braking was viewed by street racers as "sports car" stuff, maybe even "foreign" (meaning European) cars. So it might seem a bit unusual that the son of a Chevrolet dealer located in Canonsburg, Pennsylvania, outside Pittsburgh, would gravitate toward sports cars in an era when it seemed that the primary interest of American youth was beating the car in the next lane to the next stoplight. It wouldn't be a far reach to say that Donald Frank Yenko sold cars to allow him to race. Not drag racing, but road racing.

These two badges pretty much meant this was the only view of this car you were likely to see.

With his extensive road-racing background, Don Yenko made sure that Camaros bearing his name could turn and stop as well as accelerate like a scalded dog. Local Canonsburg youths were hired to install the tape graphics, pocketing $5 per car.

Yenko Chevrolet actually started when Frank Yenko started selling Durant automobiles in 1928 at Central Garage in Bentleyville, Pennsylvania. William Durant founded General Motors in 1908, and going bankrupt seemed to be part of his normal business plan. In 1932, the Great Depression forced Durant out of business, and in 1934 Frank Yenko started selling Chevrolet vehicles at Central Garage.

Business was good enough to open another Chevrolet dealership in 1949, in nearby Canonsburg. Frank Yenko placed his leading salesman, Bruno Bogdewic, in charge. The Yenko family moved to Canonsburg in 1958, and Bogdewic returned to Bentleyville, buying the original dealership. B. Bogdewic Chevrolet continues in operation to this day.

Don Yenko was born in 1927, and after graduating from Penn State and a tour in the Air Force as a meteorologist, he came back to Canonsburg to work at the family dealership. A man of many talents, he had earned his private pilot's license at age 16 and was an accomplished jazz pianist. The racing bug bit him relatively late in life, as he competed in his first race at age 30 in a Corvette. Yenko was a quick study, and trophies were soon in his house. He competed in a number of top-tier races, such as the 12 Hours of Sebring, and he was picked to replace a regular driver in the Meister Brauser Scarab at the 500-mile race at Road America in the fall of 1963. Such was his talent that he was the 1962 and 1963 SCCA B-Production National Champion driving Corvettes. It didn't hurt that Frank

Jack Douglass, a Hinsdale, Illinois, Chevrolet dealer, found out how Yenko was getting the factory to install über-high performance engines at the factory. He struck a deal with Yenko to order and outfit the cars as Yenkos at his Hinsdale dealership.

Many consider the 1969 model the high point of Camaro design, and having the Yenko treatment is frosting on the cake. The small trunk wasn't built to haul a lot of luggage, but then the Yenko Camaro hauled a different kind of cargo.

The graceful lines of the 1969 Chevelle would be replaced the following year with a beefier body style. Yenko's distinctive striping looked especially good on the curvy Chevelle.

**Above:** When brawling on Main Street USA on a Saturday night, it helps to bring a big weapon. In 1969, it didn't get any bigger in a Chevelle than the 427 found in a Yenko SC. In torque, we trust.

**Right:** While the long stripes running down the side of the Chevelle would be difficult to overlook, it wasn't hard to miss the discreet 427 badging on the front fender. Careless drivers who didn't see the engine callout competed at their own risk.

Except for the large tachometer mounted to the steering column and the Yenko graphics on the seats, the interior of the 1969 Yenko SC Chevelle was pretty much stock. With the comfortable seats and quality materials, this wasn't a bad place to spend some time.

On a dark night, one might miss that this was a 1969 Yenko SC Chevelle. The lack of body modifications meant less cost for Yenko, as he was ordering these cars relatively complete from Chevrolet. Adding graphics and wheels were about the only changes wrought in Canonsburg, PA.

Yenko was a good friend of some of the top executives at Chevrolet, and that Yenko was able to secure Gulf Oil as a primary sponsor.

As the Yenko name became increasingly familiar to the road-racing crowd, buyers who had seen the race car in action visited the small dealership for their automotive needs. Don Yenko quickly saw that selling cars and parts that appealed to road-racing enthusiasts could put money in Yenko Chevrolet's coffers. For instance, a pricing guide

to prepare a 1962 for SCCA production-car racing offered everything from disassembling and reassembling an engine with high-performance clearances, to a "built-up accelerator pedal with special hinge (for positive heel and toeing)." Yenko charged $6,143 for a competition 1962 Corvette.

In 1965, Don Yenko was racing Corvettes, but he wasn't at the front of the pack. Former racer Carroll Shelby had transformed the new Mustang into a

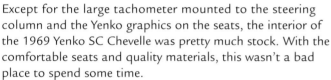

Never afraid to get his name in front of the public, Yenko mounted both his emblem and an engine callout on the rear of the 1969 Chevelle. Maybe it was to tell other drivers just what kicked their butts.

Not your normal grocery-getter, the 1969 427 Yenko Camaro was a brutal tool for getting from A to B, particularly if the two points were about a quarter-mile apart.

legitimate competition car, and with the considerable budget and backing of Ford Motor Company, victories were being racked up for the Blue Oval. Driver Mark Donohue was one of the many who grabbed the checkered flag with a Mustang, and Yenko frankly didn't like gazing at his rear bumper.

Being a Chevrolet dealer, Yenko's options were rather limited. Only one vehicle sold by the Bow Tie had, in Yenko's opinion, a chance to become a legitimate competition car, and that was the Corvair. With his history of racing Chevrolet products, he was well acquainted with the way performance support from the factory worked. Chevrolet had a little-known-to-the-public source of performance parts and vehicles known as Central Office Production Office, or COPO for short.

Fleet purchases for police agencies and taxis required vehicles outfitted with equipment not available to the public. If a dealer knew the right COPO order code, the factory would build a vehicle with equipment not normally offered. Thus the dealer was saved the time and expense of installing special parts at the dealership. Knowledge was power, as in horsepower.

For a vehicle to compete in the SCCA's production classes, it had to have a minimum production run of 100 units, so Yenko started a company separate from Yenko Chevrolet called Yenko Sports Cars Inc. Chevrolet had "officially" withdrawn from competition, so a dealer couldn't be directly involved with racing, but nothing prevented Yenko from starting a separate organization. Yenko Sports Cars Inc. would be the

Okay, so the Yenko badge looked like it was tacked on with some adhesive tape. The money a customer spent on a 427 Yenko Nova went under the hood, not on the fender.

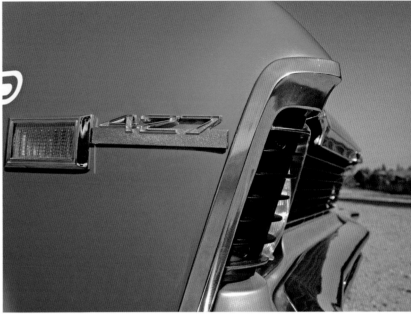

Yenko raided the Chevrolet parts bins for the engine callouts on the 1969 427 Yenko Nova. While they might have had some gaps, nobody was complaining with that monster under the hood.

producer of all of the Yenko street-performance cars in the years to come. A race shop was outfitted in the dealership, nestled between the retail showroom and the body shop. A water brake engine dynamometer and a Clayton chassis dynamometer were installed, and it wasn't long before they were put to use. Gulf Oil was a major sponsor of Yenko's racing efforts in the first half of the 1960s, and Yenko was able to use the flow benches at Gulf Oil Research in nearby Pittsburgh to fine-tune the Corvair Stinger cylinder heads.

Don Yenko knew from road racing that a lightweight vehicle with a strong engine had the best chance for taking a checkered flag. The Chevrolet Corvette was an able car, but too heavy for Yenko's taste, so he looked at what in the Chevy lineup could be turned into a successful racer. The Corvair caught his eye, with its light, unibody construction, air-cooled engine, and independent rear suspension. To that end, Yenko announced the Corvair Stinger in November 1965 and had until December 31, 1965, to build the requisite 100 cars to allow it to race in the "D" Production class.

Yenko used the COPO system to get 100 1966 Corvair Corsas built with heavy-duty suspension, M-21 four-speed manual transmission, and special steering. Then a 3.89:1 positraction differential was ordered over the counter and installed, as was a dual master brake cylinder. All of the Corvairs were painted Ermine white with black interiors. Local body shops were enlisted to paint the racing stripes down the length of the car. Mechanics at the dealership worked two shifts to finish the cars by the deadline. It was close but they made it.

The Stinger could be ordered in three levels of aggressiveness, from the street-friendly 160-horsepower, $3,278.53 Stage 1 to the SCCA race-ready, $4,099.33 220-horsepower Stage III, capable of covering the quarter-mile in 13.6 seconds at 97 mph. Better yet, it could corner like a leech. Yenko offered a Stage IV Stinger that used a slight increase in engine displacement to coax 240 horsepower from the flat-6, but it was not SCCA legal.

The Stinger was distributed by Span, Inc., out of Chicago, Illinois, and the largest number of Stingers

Simple, easy to access, and devastatingly effective, the 427-cubic-inch V-8 stuffed in the 1969 Nova made this Yenko machine, as Don Yenko himself said, "almost lethal."

With a big honking tach on the steering column and a trio of secondary gauges under the dash, the 427 Yenko Nova's interior was ready to race. While the interior might have been a bit austere, the minimalism meant light weight, a boon in competition.

was sold to Nickey Chevrolet in Chicago. Twenty-five Stingers were built in 1967, and Jerry Thompson won the D-Production national championship that year in one. Because Chevrolet discontinued the Corsa model at the end of 1966, the 1967 Corvairs ordered from Chevrolet were Monzas. These came in either Marina Blue or Bolero Red.

Yenko's race shop was a beehive of activity as the 1960s wore on. With Yenko's connections, such as Zora Arkus-Duntov, at General Motors and his history as a race-car driver, Sunray DX Oil of Oklahoma felt that backing a racing effort with Yenko could result in Sunray DX being taken as seriously as a provider of

racing lubricants. So Sunray poured money into an L88 Corvette coupe, where it was picked up at the factory in St. Louis, Missouri, and driven back to Yenko's Canonsburg dealership, where it was prepped for the race, then sent down to Florida. Don Yenko and David Morgan captured first place in the GT category and 10th overall at the 12 Hours of Sebring race.

In 1968, the same car placed first in the GT class at the 24 Hours of Daytona. Yenko would work at the dealership all week and then fly his airplane to weekend races. In late 1968, Sunray DX was acquired by Sun Oil, commonly known as Sunoco, and with Sunoco's racing deal with Roger Penske, it was felt that stepping away from Sunray DX's prior racing commitments would be in the company's best interests.

For the 1967 model year, Chevrolet's answer to the Ford Mustang, the Camaro, hit the street. Unfortunately for Bow Tie fans, corporate edict stated that midsized vehicles were limited to engines with 400-cubic-inch displacement or less. Yenko quickly saw the Camaro as a potential basis for a serious performance car, but it needed more beans beneath the hood. Dana Chevrolet and Nickey Chevrolet had worked with Anaheim, California–based Bill Thomas to stuff a 1966 Corvette 427-cubic-inch, 425-horsepower V-8 into a

The SC following the Yenko name on the side graphics stood for Street/Competition; the emphasis was clearly on competition, as a 427-cubic-inch engine in a Nova was really very street-friendly.

Novas were straight-line machines, from the styling to the way they drove. Not the most nimble vehicle in the curves, but they could sprint in a straight line like a frightened rabbit. It helped that the 427 Yenko Nova had near-locomotive grunt.

Yenko salesman Mel Bogus drove this demonstrator around the Midwest region, calling on every Chevrolet dealer he could find in an attempt to sell them one, two, or more Yenko Sports Cars. The demonstration ride was fast and usually got the dealer's attention.

1967 Camaro, and Don Yenko tapped that knowledge by using Thomas as a source of performance equipment such as headers and traction bars.

Yenko built 54 "Super Camaros" in 1967, all of them equipped with four-speed manual transmissions and dealer-installed complete 427-cubic-inch engines. Famed drag-racer Dick Harrell cherry-picked the components that were used in the "Yenko Super Camaro," such as the rear-end ratios, transmission, exhaust, and clutch. Depending on the wishes of the buyer, the Yenko Super Camaro could be outfitted for use on the street, strip, or anywhere in between. Camaros destined for use in competition were advertised as being tested on the track or strip. Standard Chevrolet Camaro 350s would

be shipped to Yenko's dealership, where the small-block would be pulled and a crate big-block would fill the space. Equipment specified by the customer would then be installed and the car tested before delivery. All it took was money.

In order to maximize the number of vehicles that he could sell, Yenko concentrated considerable resources to do something few other performance dealers would undertake: creating a nationwide distribution system. He had salesmen visit dealers with demonstrator Yenko vehicles, usually a Camaro. By showing dealers the history of the Yenko brand and giving them a neck-stretching ride, he'd sign up yet another dealer. Salesmen tried to sell six vehicles in the same general

Yenko tended to keep the interiors of his cars relatively stock, just applying YSC stickers to the headrests. The placement was rather clever, as headrests are usually the most visible part of an interior from outside the vehicle.

area, allowing a full transporter to hit all of the dealerships in the same trip, saving costs. Yet big dealers weren't ignored; in fact, they were brought into the fold. Outfits such as Chicago's Nickey Chevrolet and Los Angeles–based Dana Chevrolet were Yenko outlets.

Yenko figured that he had to reduce the cost of fitting the Camaro with a 427 for 1968, and he hit upon it by ordering the cars with the high-performance 396. Then at the dealership he would replace the 396 with a 427 shortblock, meaning he would change out the block, piston, and connecting rods and crankshaft. On top of the new parts, the original heads, intake manifold, and carburetor were installed, as well as ancillary parts such as starters, alternators, and the water pump. With fewer parts needing to be replaced, costs were saved. The mechanics who were converting the cars

By astute manipulation of the COPO system, Yenko was able to get Chevrolet to install the potent 427 engine into the smallish Camaro at the factory, saving him time and money by eliminating the need to install a replacement engine. Functional cowl induction kept the big-block inhaling copious amounts of fresh air.

There wasn't room for many more badges on the panel between the taillights, but for the owner, these were the badges to display. Yenko cars weren't cheap, everyone knew it, and the owner wanted to ensure everyone knew that he wrote the check.

The handsome cowl induction hood debuted in 1969 and served a dual purpose: feeding cool ambient air into the engine's induction system and providing an ideal place for Yenko to mount graphics. It's doubtful that Chevrolet's stylists had that in mind when they designed the hood.

Yenko saw that his method of assembly was limiting the number of high-performance automobiles he could sell. And never forget, Yenko was in the business of selling cars. Don Yenko approached Chevrolet about the possibility of having the factory install 427-cubic-inch V-8s. This would minimize the work at the dealership level and allow Yenko to sell more vehicles more quickly, as well as send order cars to other dealers. Chevy agreed if Yenko promised to keep it a secret.

into 427 Yenko Camaros were paid $140 for each vehicle they could complete. A technician working fast could finish the transformation in one day. Sixty-eight Yenko Camaros were built.

Word had quickly spread that the Yenko Camaros were fast, and their desirability meant more customers.

Yenko started to really work the COPO system in 1969 when he would order Camaros as L78 396 cars, then Chevrolet would fit the Camaro with heavy-duty

Traditionally, Novas are rather barren of swoopy styling, instead displaying simple, straight lines. The graphics package fitted onto the 1970 Yenko Nova Deuce eschewed fancy patterns; rather it emphasized the clean design of the vehicle.

Yenko called the 1970 Nova a "Deuce," as the full Chevrolet name of the vehicle had been Chevy II. Hence the Deuce moniker on the leading edge of the hood.

suspension components such as a 1-inch front antiroll bar and E70X15 bias-ply tires on Rally wheels, a bigger carburetor, and a 140-mph speedometer under the auspices of COPO #9737, the "Sports Car Conversion."

Under the hood, COPO #9561 was used, resulting in a 427-cubic-inch engine being fitted between the shock towers. The Rat powerplant could be bolted to either an M-22 four-speed manual tranny or a three-speed automatic. With the manual, the engine used solid valve lifters, while automatic transmission-equipped cars found hydraulic lifters inside the iron-block bruiser. The 1969 cars started to arrive at Yenko in January 1969, and they went to a

warehouse that Yenko had rented across the creek behind the dealership.

Buyers could choose to have the famous Yenko stripes deleted, but most wanted to flaunt what they had. Vehicles destined for the graphics were taken down the road to a large field, where local teens, including

For 1970, Yenko fitted the lightweight Nova with an LT-1 350-cubic-inch engine sourced from the Corvette. Rated at 360 horsepower, it lived to rev, and in the Nova, the engine's light weight meant improved handling.

Yenko chose Hurst wheels as much for their stylish looks as their durability. Enormously strong, they weren't the lightest wheels on the market, but they were virtually indestructible.

Mounting a hood tachometer gave any car a street-fighter look. It helped that the LT-1 engine beneath the tach was strong, and combined with the diminutive Nova platform, it didn't take long for the tach needle to swing toward the north end of the scale.

The Yenko Deuce exuded a purposeful, no-nonsense air, like a strong machine waiting to be put to work. The tape stripes were tasteful, unlike many of the other performance machines of the era.

Yenko's daughter, Lynn, were paid $5 per car to apply the stripes. Years before, the field had been the site of Standard Chemical Company, which worked with uranium and rare metals, as well as supplying Madame Curie with radium. Then in 1942, Vitro Chemical Works took over the spot. This firm worked with uranium ore

There's nothing like a discreet badge to call attention to a car. Most people tend to think of Camaros and Chevelles as Yenko creations, but his Novas were some of the fastest cars he built.

for the World War II Manhattan Project. Over time, considerable radioactive materials found their way into the soil. After Vitro shut down, a pottery plant used the land and clay to produce their pottery. To this day, Canonsburg pottery can be detected with a Geiger counter. Into this field the Yenko Camaros were sent for striping.

To Yenko, the COPO process saved him money in ways other than not needing to install the L72 engine at the dealership. In 1967 and 1968, he had to pay General Motors for warranty coverage for each of the converted cars. With a vehicle intended for abuse, it could get pricey. But with the introduction of the COPO cars for 1969, the factory now assumed warranty responsibility. That was a significant load off of

Don Yenko was a very good road race driver, yet he knew that drag racing was not his best skill set. So he tapped one of the best drivers to ever grace a quarter-mile: Dick Harrell. With lightning-quick reflexes and quality cars from Yenko, he was a real force to be reckoned with. *Author Collection*

Yenko's salesmen would travel the country, driving from dealer to dealer, lining up enough sold cars in a region to justify loading up a transporter for the trip. The truck wouldn't make the journey with just one or two vehicles; it had to be full to make the trip worthwhile. *Author Collection*

Yenko's shoulders. Yet Yenko still needed to tap old friend Vince Piggins at General Motors to fend off vocal dealers when raucous Yenko products would roll into their service departments. They didn't believe that Chevrolet would actually build such a car.

Now that he had streamlined the process of having Camaros equipped with 427 engines built by the factory, he could move more cars. Production in 1969 resulted in 198 Camaros being "converted." Yenko turned his attention to a couple of other vehicles in the Chevrolet lineup, the Chevelle and Nova. It wasn't difficult to use the COPO system to have L-72 big-block engines installed in the Chevelle SS396. Only 99 were built, using the #9562 and #9737 COPO codes.

But try as he might, Don Yenko couldn't get Chevrolet to install the L72 427-cubic-inch engine in the lightweight Nova. Something about liability. So his dealership had to pull the engine out of the stock Nova and slip the Corvette-based powerplant into the engine

bay. The result was a car that Don Yenko described in an April 1987 *Muscle Car Review* interview as "a beast, it was almost lethal. I was worried about that car; it was not for amateurs. I really was skirting the edge of product liability with that car."

As the 1969 model year wound toward its end, the sky came crashing in on Don Yenko, and every other performance dealer, in the form of insurance. Yenko found that he was having difficulty selling the ground-pounders due to rocketing insurance rates. Many buyers could afford the car, or the insurance, but not both. So bad was the shortage of customers that Yenko thought about pulling the 427-cubic-inch engines out of the remaining cars and installing leftover 396 engines. Fortunately for Yenko, the remaining cars finally sold. But the future was going to be shaped by the insurance companies.

When the 1970 Yenko high-performance lineup was introduced, many were shocked by the absence of the Camaro and Chevelle. Only one car was being sold under

Don Yenko felt that the Corvair was a valid platform for a competitive racing machine. He felt that the Corvette was too expensive for the normal enthusiast, and nobody else was using the Corvair for racing. Yenko transformed the Corvair into a legitimate winner. *Mark Gillespie*

Don Yenko (left) smiles for the camera as he poses with one of the dealers who signed up to distribute Yenko Sports Cars. The sign is misleading, as Yenko didn't build anywhere close to 350 Camaros in 1969, but a little stretching of the truth made for better public relations. *Lynn Shelton-Zoiopoulos Collection*

Don Yenko was a top-shelf road racer, competing in Corvettes in endurance races such as Sebring and Le Mans. *Lynn Shelton-Zoiopoulos Collection*

After Don Yenko moved his Chevrolet dealership from the diminutive building in Canonsburg, Pennsylvania, he picked up a Subaru franchise, and it was headquartered in the old building. *Lynn Shelton-Zoiopoulos Collection*

the banner of performance, and it was actually flying under the radar. Yenko figured that if he wanted to sell muscle, he'd have to hide it in a bread-and-butter car. Enter the Nova 350. Shoppers from coast to coast depended on the small-block Nova to get to work, for shopping, and school. Except for the monster big-block Novas that Yenko sold in 1969, nobody gave the Nova a first look, much less a second. That was the beauty of Yenko's idea.

By utilizing the COPO system again and checking #9010 and #9737 on the order form, the stock grocery-getter 350 normally found in a basic Nova was replaced with a solid-lifter LT-1 350/360-horsepower engine and the Sports Car Conversion package. The final product combined a lightweight platform with a potent, flexible engine, and the resulting $3,993 car sold well, to the tune of 175 units, making it the biggest-selling Yenko Super Car. Better yet, it was insurable as a "Nova 350." As it was a result of the COPO pipeline, it carried a factory warranty, much to Yenko's relief.

As a full-line Chevrolet dealer, Don Yenko could see the writing on the performance wall. The factory was dropping engine compression ratios faster than a hot

potato, and performance models were starting to be a bit less earth-shaking. Yet the racer in Yenko needed an outlet, and he felt that the new Vega could combine the virtues of light weight and a strong engine to produce a worthy successor to the Corvair Stinger.

In fact, Yenko named the resulting car the Vega Stinger II. He planned to build 500 copies, thus qualifying the car to race in the SCCA's D/Production class. The diminutive car was to be fitted with a 155-horsepower turbocharged engine, but the government interceded. The government mandated that to change a factory engine's emission controls required a 50,000-mile durability test. Yenko tallied up how much it would cost and decided to step away from offering a turn-key package to the public. Instead, he tossed the turbo kit into the trunk, with installation directions for the owner included. In truth, few were built. The Vega soon revealed itself as a rolling stool sample, with problems ranging from short-lived, oil-burning engines to terminal rust.

With Chevrolet out of the performance business, Yenko took his business in new directions. He still

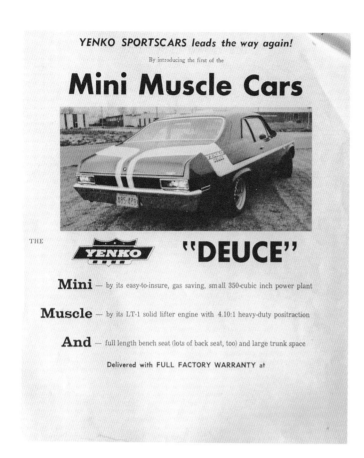

Yenko saw that the muscle-car market was going to start leaning toward more sane levels of engine performance, and in 1970 his LT-1 350-cubic-inch-equipped Nova hit the street. Even Yenko admitted that the 427-equipped Novas of 1969 were over the top. *Author Collection*

operated a thriving high-performance catalog business, but he started to diversify his automotive holdings with the opening of a new Chevrolet dealership in McMurray, Pennsylvania, in 1972. The old buildings in Canonsburg became a Porsche/Audi/Fiat dealership, but that fizzled out. After that, Saab was the nameplate on the sign, but that too failed to succeed. Next up for the buildings was Yenko Performance and Marine, but finally that was closed up and the buildings sold.

In 1981 Yenko rolled out another performance car, one that could mesh the desire for a thrilling ride while still preserving street-legal status. He used the 1981 Camaro Z-28 as a basis, and the heart was a turbocharged 350-cubic-inch engine. Named the Turbo Z, it came in two levels, Stage I, which had the turbo, special hood, dual exhaust, and graphics, and Stage II, which included all of the Stage I equipment as

well as special Koni shocks, seats, wheels, tires, and other upscale bits. Only 19 units were built, and Yenko took it as a sign that the performance days were well and truly over.

Don Yenko still had a hand in the car business, as he owned Yenko Subaru in Pittsburgh/Dormont and Yenko Honda in McMurray. In 1986 Don Yenko was in negotiations with Jaguar and Hyundai about opening dealerships in the Pittsburgh area. Unfortunately, as he was landing his Cessna 210M at Charleston, West Virginia, on March 5, 1987, he lost control, crashing the aircraft, killing Yenko and three passengers.

Without doubt, Don Yenko advanced the performance of Chevrolet products to a degree matched by few. A talented competitor, a strong entrepreneur, and a true performance enthusiast, the muscle car community was richer with Donald Yenko on the scene.

# CHAPTER 10

# HURST

## *SHIFTERS, GIRLS, AND MARKETING*

In today's society, it's generally acknowledged that in order to succeed, you need a college degree, and if possible, more than one. Yet there have been people who have made significant impacts, yet never finished high school. They haven't been taught that they couldn't do something. George Hurst was one of those gifted individuals who could put his ideas into reality, and then market it for all it was worth. His best-known invention was a staple on virtually every muscle car ever made, and his name was synonymous with quality. But Hurst wasn't a one-trick pony; he created products that are still in wide use today, including the item that ties all real muscle cars together—the Hurst shifter.

Hurst partnered with a number of manufacturers in the 1960s and '70s. No partnership was more famous than the venture with Oldsmobile.

Oldsmobile stylists did a masterful job crafting the 1969 4-4-2, and when Hurst entered the picture, the drama quotient was raised considerably.

Hurst and Oldsmobile teamed up to create some of the most memorable vehicles of the entire muscle car era. The rear wing was mostly for show, but it toughened up the Cutlass-based vehicle. At the other end of the car, the 455-cubic-inch engine did wonders.

Hurst was born in New York City in 1927 and spent his youth in Little Ferry, New Jersey. Before he could graduate from high school, he enlisted in the U.S. Navy and became an aviation machinist's mate. The mechanical skills he learned working on high-performance aircraft would be put to use when he left the service in 1954. Settling in Philadelphia, he opened George Hurst Automotive, where he handled regular auto repairs, restorations, and engine swaps. Customers would come in with big cars from the 1940s, but the period engines didn't have the power of the contemporary engines. Hurst would pull the old mill out and replace it with a healthy new Buick or Oldsmobile engine. Because the newer driveline usually differed in its mounting and shift linkage from the

Dual scoops on the leading edge of the hood actually fed cool air into the induction system, as well as provided a great place to position engine callout graphics.

original, Hurst would need to fabricate a new shifter and motor mounts. He quickly found out what worked and what didn't. An engineer, Bill Campbell, was hired to assist in creating in metal what Hurst would dream up. Compared with the factory components, Hurst's units tended to be over engineered.

With examples of his motor mounts and shifters, he headed to Detroit in late December 1958, to Gratiot Auto Supply, a performance parts shop. The management at Gratiot took a pass on Hurst's motor mounts, but they were enthusiastic about the shifters. Hurst was told that they could sell as many shifters as he could build. Continuing his journey west, he headed to California, where more interest in the shifters made it clear to Hurst that there was real money to be made. Hightailing it back to Philly, he borrowed $20,000 and set to work tooling up to fill the orders.

Word quickly spread about the seemingly bullet-proof shifters. *Hot Rod* magazine ran a feature on the new Hurst shifter, and performance enthusiasts started clamoring for it. Before long, racers were starting to install

Hurst shifters, confident that their next shift would be a clean one. One of the *Hot Rod* readers was Assistant Chief Engineer John DeLorean, and he notified E. M. "Pete" Estes, then the chief engineer at Pontiac, that this Hurst shifter was worth a look. Hurst was asked to meet Estes and his boss, Semon "Bunkie" Knudsen, and soon an arrangement was made that allowed the Hurst shifter to be sold as a factory option. Pontiac was big into racing in the early 1960s, and by using Hurst shifters, the factory gained immediate street credibility. The Hurst shifter was available as an over-the-counter unit for the Catalinas starting in 1961, and running through 1963 it was standard equipment with the potent 421-cubic-inch Super Duty engine.

Within a couple of years, all of Detroit's muscle car manufacturers offered Hurst shifters as an option. Then in 1964, Pontiac introduced the mass-market GTO, equipped with a Hurst shifter *right from the factory!* That kind of quality component on a showroom car spoke volumes to the performance enthusiasts who were snapping up The Great Ones. With the release of

While many didn't give American Motors a first look, much less a second, the fact is, with the Rambler's light weight and the 390-cubic-inch V-8's power, the SC/Rambler was a hot little car. The red, white, and blue "A" paint option made sure everyone knew it.

American Motors felt that they couldn't beat the big boys from Detroit, so they compensated with sheer cheek. The wild styling and flamboyant paint and graphic scheme put the SC/Rambler in another world.

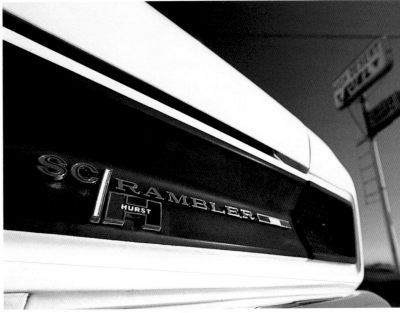

Hurst was an equal-opportunity performance enhancer. American Motors needed a known performance name to gain instant street credibility, and Hurst was pleased to work with a company that listened to fresh ideas. The result was unlike anything from Detroit.

Some American Motors dealers were complaining that the original wild paint scheme of the SC/Ramblers was attracting the wrong kind of attention, and they were having a tough time selling the cars. So AMC changed the look to something a touch more subdued. *Mike Mueller*

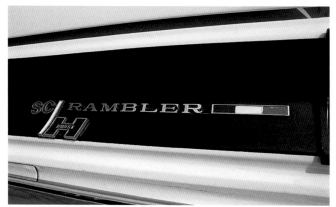

Hurst was a master of promotion, but the SC/Rambler is one of the company's lesser-known efforts. On the drag strip, one of these little stormers could crank out low-14-second runs. *Mike Mueller*

**Left:** Not much was done to the interior of the SC/Rambler to upgrade it. Dangle a big honkin' tachometer and a beefy Hurst shifter in front of a performance junkie and he'll bite. *Mike Mueller*

By the time Chrysler and Hurst teamed up to create a high-performance version of the venerable 300 Hurst, the car was a nondescript highway cruiser. With Hurst in the picture, the result was a visually exciting car, a difficult task with a full-size platform.

While the hood scoop was for show only, it provided an excellent location for callouts touting the collaboration between Chrysler and Hurst.

the sporty GTO, anyone could lay their hands on the finest shifter on the market.

George Hurst had become good friends with Wally Parks, the founder of the NHRA, and over the years, Hurst would support the organization in both financial and marketing efforts. Hurst, one of the most flamboyant marketers in the automotive world, knew that getting the Hurst name in front of racing enthusiasts would translate into exposure and sales. Pretty girls always garner attention, and starting in 1962, Miss Hurst Shifter made her appearance. Actually, a number of women were employed, starting with Hurst's second wife. Then as the title became Miss Hurst Golden Shifter, a succession of women such as Pat Flannery, June Cochran, and starting in 1966, the most famous, Linda Vaughn, were inducted. At hundreds of events across the globe, these representatives presented the Hurst Company in an eye-catching, youthful manner.

George Hurst used special automobiles to catch the eye as well. Jack "Doc" Watson, an engineer who could

American Motors hoped to carry the momentum from the SC/Rambler into 1970 with a follow-up performance car, the Rebel Machine. *Mike Mueller*

get things done, had opened a door between Hurst and General Motors in the early 1960s, and Hurst used him to develop drag-strip exhibition vehicles. Some of his efforts were the 1966 twin-engine 4-4-2 hardtop, "Hurst Hairy Oldsmobile," and even a Chrysler product, the 1965 Barracuda "Hemi Under Glass."

The success of those cars in spreading the Hurst name encouraged Hurst to task Watson with creating a special 1968 Olds 4-4-2, equipped with a huge 455-cubic-inch V-8. The resulting Hurst/Olds was the first in a long line of collaborative efforts between Hurst and the General Motors division. General Motors had a corporate edict that engines larger than 400 cubic inches would not be installed in intermediate platforms. Hurst saw that the engine compartment had plenty of room for a bigger engine, so out came the "little" 400 and in slipped a strong 455. Of course, Hurst couldn't do things half way, and the 1968 Hurst/Olds sported a special two-tone

paint scheme, Hurst shifter, and Ram-Air functional hood scoops. With 390 horsepower and a tire-shredding 500 lb-ft of torque, the H/O was a plush monster. Olds wasn't the only GM nameplate that got together with Hurst; Pontiac was allied with Hurst starting in 1961 and continued the relationship into the 1970's.

Proving the 1968 Hurst/Olds wasn't a one-year treat, Hurst and Olds upped the ante in 1969 with an even more outrageous car. Based again on the Cutlass platform, the 455-equipped car sported a special Ram Air hood with aggressive scoops, a huge full-width rear spoiler, two-tone white and gold paint, and a slew of emblems. This was one extroverted vehicle.

In 1970, there wasn't a standalone Hurst/Olds vehicle, as Oldsmobile felt that maybe the "right" corporate image wasn't being presented. Olds took the planned '70 H/O that Hurst had designed and released it as a Rallye 350 instead.

American Motors completely ignored the performance market in the early and mid-1960s, relying on a sturdy but unremarkable 390-cubic-inch V-8 rated at 340 horsepower to motivate its so-called performance. AMC hadn't invested any money in a true performance powerplant, so when the company decided to release a street fighter, the 390 was the only option. *Mike Mueller*

It might be said that Oldsmobile saw the error of its ways and decided to introduce a 1972 Hurst/Olds. Aiding its exposure was its starring role as the Pace Car for the 1972 Indianapolis 500 race. In production car form, the H/O could be had as either a coupe or a convertible. It was a success, and Oldsmobile continued to provide vehicles for Hurst to massage.

In 1973, General Motors introduced a new A-body platform among its divisions, and Oldsmobile used its version, the Cutlass, as the basis for another H/O. Equipped with the requisite Hurst Dual Gate shifter, a 455 engine, and colorful paint, there were over 1,000 built for 1973. This was a real success for a boutique car.

A Hurst/Olds again paced the 1974 Indy 500, and it used the biggest engine in Oldsmobile's catalog, the 455,

When auto manufacturers wanted to tap into the increasingly affluent youth market, they occasionally released vehicles with interiors that the car makers thought "spoke" to the Mod Crowd. The results were often embarrassingly tacky. At least the Hurst shifter was the real deal. *Mike Mueller*

Much the same approach was taken in 1983, when the 15th-Anniversary Hurst/Olds were rolled out. However, Detroit in general, and Oldsmobile in particular, was figuring out how to extract horsepower from the company's engines while meeting fuel and emission standards. The two-tone black and silver Cutlass-based car packed a 307-cubic-inch V-8 and used a new Hurst shifter, called the Lightning Rods. With a trio of sticks jutting out of the center console, the shifter was designed to improve the shifting under hard acceleration. While its effectiveness at that task was questionable, it certainly was a head-turner, and it got people talking about Olds and Hurst in a favorable fashion.

Due to the public's response to the 1983 H/O, it was only right that the package was again offered in '84. About the only change was the paint scheme; the original silver and black combo was resurrected for 1984. Yet Oldsmobile stepped away from the H/O the following year. It wasn't until 1988 that the next, and last, Hurst/Olds was released. This was to be the last year for the rear-drive Cutlass Calais platform, so Oldsmobile celebrated the 20th anniversary of the original H/O. Four vehicles were built by "Doc" Watson. After the cars were built, kits were made available to retrofit onto customer cars. That ended the relationship between Hurst and Oldsmobile.

Oldsmobile was not the only General Motors division that enjoyed a positive working partnership with Hurst. Pontiac had started the use of Hurst shifters in the 1961 Super Duty Catalinas and then expanded into the GTO. In the early 1970s, the SSJ Hurst/Grand Prix was released, complete with vivid two-tone paint and Hurst badging. Options included special wheels, a sunroof, a Hurst Auto/Stick Shifter, even a digital computer that monitored fuel economy.

Giving away automobiles isn't normally the best way to forward a company's best interests, but Hurst did just that, many times. Race winners across the country would often find the keys to a Hurst automobile

and like any proper Hurst automobile, it was laden with products from Hurst. Oldsmobile even tapped Hurst to work its magic on a number of Delta Royale 88 convertibles. Most were outfitted with the 455 engine and wore the traditional white and gold Hurst colors.

Once again, Oldsmobile dove into the Hurst pool in 1975, selling the H/O with both a 350-cubic-inch V-8 as well as the 455 powerplant. As the country was deeply mired in the "gas crisis," straight-line acceleration wasn't exactly emphasized, but for the period, the H/O displayed adequate performance in a comfortable vehicle.

It wasn't until 1979 when the next iteration of the Hurst/Olds was released. Primarily a heavily contented Cutlass, it was given a healthy dose of Hurst graphics and sporty wheels to convey the look, if not the ability, of a street bruiser.

The Grand Prix was built on the same basic substructure as the Chevrolet Monte Carlo. Even so, the Pontiac version seemed to be a larger car and possessed ideal proportions.

Hurst Grand Prix production relied on standard Grand Prix SSJs, but the prototype was constructed on a Type J platform.

This is a re-creation of the original Hurst Grand Prix. Owned by Pontiac guru Jim Wangers, it shows what the vehicle looked like as it was presented to the Pontiac decision makers.

Two paint schemes were available in 1973 for the Hurst/Olds, white/gold and black/gold. Oldsmobile released the new A-body in 1973, and the relationship between the carmaker and Hurst was a success. *Mike Mueller*

The H/O emblem on the rear was, in 1973, widely respected in enthusiast circles. Production that year was 1,097 units. *Mike Mueller*

in their hands after a significant victory. Contest winners were often presented with Hurst autos, such as the famous gold Hurst GTO that went to a 19-year-old, Alex Lampone, who had counted how many times the word "tiger" was sung in the hit song "GeeTO Tiger" (42) and penned a 25-word essay explaining why he would like the car. High-profile promotions like this went far in spreading the Hurst name.

Lest you think that General Motors was the only manufacturer that used the Hurst line of shifters, the crosstown competition used Hurst products as well. Ford and Chrysler installed Hurst shifters in their performance cars, including the Mustang, Torino, Road Runner, Charger, and a score of other muscle-car nameplates.

With the passing of true high-performance, the H/O started to lean more heavily on luxury appointments, including swivel bucket seats, which were ideal for maintaining a lady's dignity when exiting the stylish cruiser. *Mike Mueller*

Granted, compression was reduced in an effort to reach the government's emission regulations, but 455 cubic inches still makes for a big engine. And one of the benefits of a big engine is big torque. It was child's play to lay waste to the rear tires. *Mike Mueller*

For the 1970 model year, the Chrysler 300-Hurst was introduced. It wore white and gold paint, had gold accents, and had a large rear wing, which was rather unusual on a full-size car. Under the hood, a 440-cubic-inch V-8 helped the monster get under way. Over 500 were built.

Even American Motors jumped onto the Hurst bandwagon with the release of the 1969 Hurst S/C Rambler. Built on the lightweight Rambler, a vehicle with a reputation so pedestrian that it was a joke, the S/C Rambler went way in the other direction to show that American Motors knew what performance was. Under the tall, funky hood scoop lay AMC's 390-cubic-inch engine, a 315-horsepower V-8 that, at first glance, didn't seem like it could compete with larger displacement engines. But the key to the car's performance was the featherweight Rambler itself, which gave the Hurst S/C Rambler real

Only one transmission was available in the 1973 H/O—the highly regarded Turbo Hydra-Matic 400 three-speed automatic. Hurst's Dual Gate floor-mounted shifter handled gear selection duties, allowing the driver to put the tranny in drive and forget about it, or pick the specific gears. *Mike Mueller*

Any Hurst/Olds production car had plenty of identification that this was not your father's Oldsmobile. A Mylar insert in the quarter windows was another clue if someone missed the special paint. *Mike Mueller*

performance. It could sprint down the quarter-mile in the low-14-second range at 100 mph. Not bad for a car with a reputation as a grandma's ride.

In 1970, AMC dropped the S/C Rambler but replaced it with the Rebel Machine, built on the midsized Rebel SST sport model. It packed the same 390 engine used the year before, but the public essentially ignored it. The Hurst S/C Rambler succeeded because it was just quirky enough, and fast enough. But the Machine was simply a tarted-up Rebel. For once, the Hurst name wasn't enough to save a boring car.

George Hurst continued to build his business, acquiring clutch-maker Schiefer Manufacturing and brake-system-builder Airheart in the mid-1960s. However, in 1968, George Hurst took his company public, and in 1970, Hurst was bought out by Sunbeam, maker of household appliances. George was promised a seat on the board of directors and an executive position, but neither came to pass.

Hurst, always thinking of new products, developed a portable hydraulic device in 1972 that would have a profound effect on the public: the "Jaws of Life." This invention

The taillight treatment was reminiscent of the 1969 H/O 455. Dual exhausts helped the 1973 H/O produce an impressive rumble from its 455-cubic-inch V-8. *Mike Mueller*

Oldsmobile was tapped to pace the Indianapolis 500-mile race in 1974, and at the head of the pack was the H/O. It was based on the Cutlass S coupe. Approximately 1,800 H/Os were built in 1974. *Mike Mueller*

In 1974, two engines were offered in the H/O, a 455-cubic-inch bruiser and a 350-cubic-inch V-8. But if you were a California buyer, the small-block was your only choice, as the Golden State's strict emission regulations kept the big-block off of California Olds dealers' showroom floors. *Mike Mueller*

is now in worldwide use by emergency personnel, and it has aided in the saving of hundreds of lives. At the time of its development, Sunbeam wanted nothing to do with the invention and told George Hurst to drop it. Refusing to set it aside, he continued to refine it. Shortly after that, George Hurst was "eased" out of the company bearing his name.

From then to his death in 1986, George Hurst was involved with a number of ventures, some more successful than others, but none coming close to the massive success of his shifters. Yet today, Hurst shifters are still the standard for stout, reliable gear changing. Enthusiasts then and now realized that a muscle car, regardless of manufacturer, had to have a Hurst shifter, or it was just a pretender.

Oldsmobile wasn't above resurrecting a historic name if it would give a new product street credibility. That was the case with the application of the W-30 package in the 1974 H/O. *Mike Mueller*

A reminder of times past, the hood ornament on the 1974 H/O was a subtle touch from a carmaker that pursued an up-market audience. *Mike Mueller*

For 1974, the H/O had a revised rear, with the taillights now flush with the bodywork and a federally mandated bumper. Anything but subtle, it kept the Hurst name in front of a mainstream audience. *Mike Mueller*

In the early 1970s the Oldsmobile Cutlass was one of the most popular nameplates in America, and the collaboration between Hurst and Olds put a true performance flavor on General Motors' stylish A-body platform. *Mike Mueller*

# CHAPTER 11

# SHELBY AMERICAN

## AMERICAN MUSCLE, VIA ENGLAND

Many get into the business of selling cars to get into racing. But Texan Carroll Shelby entered the world of selling vehicles after he had climbed to the top of Sports Car racing. To put a touch of drama on things, his doctor told him that he had months to live.

That was in 1959, and he's still playing with fast cars. His life story would make one hell of a movie. Shelby, and the cars that he designed, built, and sold, are larger than life, and his influence cannot be understated. If anyone could be the poster boy for "been there, done that," it's Shelby.

Externally, the Cobra roadster deviated little from its original AC Ace roots. The real difference from the Ace was the installation of the Ford V-8 engine.

Shelby paid AC $1,500 for each rolling body/chassis. It took 22 panels to create one body.

Shelby came into the racing world at an age when today's "stars" are hanging up their driving suits. At 29, he passed his days as a chicken farmer. But in 1952, he got behind the wheel of an MG TC, and won the first two races he competed in. The following year, he won a race in his bib overalls, setting himself apart from any other competitors. As he continued to collect trophies, he moved up into ever-more-powerful cars and higher-profile races. His high-water mark as a driver was at the wheel of an Aston Martin DBR1, when he and co-driver Roy Salvadori won the 1959 24 Hours of Le Mans race.

Unknown to virtually everyone, Shelby was suffering from a heart ailment, angina pectoris, which required him to slip nitroglycerine tablets under his tongue to keep the pain in check. He was using the medication while driving at Le Mans but refused to tell anyone for fear he would be yanked from the team. In 1960, the doctors told him that his driving career was over. Many would have taken this as a sign to scale back and take things easy. But Carroll Shelby was not like the many.

Cobra occupants enjoyed intimate seating, thanks to an interior that was previntage British sports car. This 1965 Cobra sold new for approximately $5,995.

In the 1960s, when Corvette racers got this view in their mirrors, they knew their goose was cooked. With a surplus of power and a dearth of weight, the Cobra seemed to defy the laws of physics.

Voluptuous fenders had bulged dramatically to cover the ever-growing tires, which were necessary as increasingly powerful engines were installed. Yet the bigger rubber was still easily overcome with a flexing of the foot.

That same year, Lee Iacocca became a vice president at Ford Motor Company, and at age 36, he wanted to see that Ford would have an impact on the infant performance market. Together with a group of eight Ford managers, this "Fairlane Committee" crafted a plan to inject various Ford automobiles with the verve then lacking in the company's lineup. "Total Performance" was the umbrella that covered the performance effort. Granted, the AMA ban in 1957 was meant to shackle the auto manufacturers from competing in sanctioned races, but General Motors and Chrysler were blowing the ban into the weeds with their thinly veiled race efforts.

By 1962, Ford had wrapped up development of a lightweight V-8 engine, displacing 221 cubic inches. Shelby, who knew people at Ford, got an engine and

With the huge 427-cubic-inch engine in the nose, rapid handling was not the big-block Cobra's forte. Rather, it was happier lunging from corner to corner in frightening bursts of speed.

dropped it into an AC Ace, a small two-seat British sports car that was powered by a Bristol 2-liter straight-six. The Blue Oval transplant was a simple way to inject the vehicle with additional power at modest cost. This would be the formula that Shelby would use for the rest of his career.

In short order, the little 221 engine would grow to 260 cubic inches, and ultimately grow again to displace 289 cubes. Shelby worked out an arrangement, something he has always been skilled at, to bring engineless AC Aces into the United States, to his shop in Los Angeles. There, Ford small-block V-8s would be installed. The resulting car was called the Cobra, and marketing-savvy Shelby made sure the new car got plenty of press by tapping some of his friends in the automotive publishing business.

But Shelby wasn't content to merely sell his new sports car; this was a man who had won at Le Mans. Ford didn't have anything that could compete, but they backed Shelby. In no time, Cobras were found at racetracks across the country where, frankly, they kicked everyone's ass. Chevrolet had recently introduced its beautiful 1963 Sting Ray, equipped with a wide range of healthy engines and independent rear suspension. The Cobras ate the 'Vettes for breakfast.

It didn't take long for Shelby to realize that Dean Moon's shop, where the first Cobras were built, wasn't going to work as a production facility. He moved into Lance Reventlow's former shop at Princeton and Carter Streets in Venice, California, when Reventlow stepped away from building sports cars. Soon the new buildings were buzzing with activity, including the fitment of Ford's new 427 NASCAR engine into the diminutive sports car. The result was a lethally fast racer, totally

With nary a misplaced line, the purity of the original AC Ace was still visible, even in 427 guise. While some sports cars could be compared to a rapier, the big-block Cobra was your basic sledgehammer.

Lacking only a number, the 427 Cobra was a race car that could be driven, barely, on the street. With the curvaceous aluminum bodywork, care had to be taken not to dent the malleable metal.

unforgiving of mistakes. But the Cobra program proved to Ford that the Texan knew his way around the car business.

Lee Iacocca and the Fairlane Committee came up with a lot of ideas, the most successful being essentially a rebody of the economical, but visually boring, Falcon. The Mustang hit the scene in April 1964, to widespread acclaim. Yet it was, in Shelby's words, "a secretary's car." Cute, inexpensive, and not terribly fast, the Mustang sold well, but Ford wanted to do more.

Taking a page from the Cobra playbook, they approached Shelby with orders to transform the performance of the Mustang from adequate to thrilling. So he did just what he'd done with the AC Ace: inject more beans beneath the hood, upgrade the suspension, and then take it out to a race track. The result was the 1965 Shelby GT350. And like the Cobra, it was a dominant force on the track.

Carroll Shelby had a half-dozen 1966 GT350 convertibles built as gifts to friends and family. They were never intended to be sold new to the public. The wily Texan kept this example for himself.

Only 34 Shelby GT350Rs were built in 1965 and were meant for off-road usage only. All were destined for the race track.

To fit the wheel/tire package, the wheel openings were slightly flared and enlarged to provide clearance. A quick-fill gas cap was located inside the trunk, requiring the trunk lid to be opened to fuel the car.

With the name Shelby on every car, it was no surprise that a proper Shelby race team was formed. Starting in the early 1960s and on into the latter part of the decade, there were few motorsports venues that Shelby didn't compete in, and win. From drag racing, to endurance contests, Shelby hired the best talent available and then got out of the way. Some of the more notable venues that Shelby won at include Sebring, Le Mans, and Bridgehampton. It didn't hurt that Shelby, the original charmer, had close ties with various highly placed Ford executives, including Don Frey, Leo Beebe, and Peyton Cramer. Cramer became Shelby's general manager, and the lessons he learned at Shelby American were put to use later at a Chevrolet dealership in Los Angeles.

Shelby American distributed Cobras at its headquarters, as well as at various Ford dealerships across the country. One of the biggest Shelby outlets was Tasca Ford in Rhode Island. Not only would Ford dealers sell Shelby cars such as the Cobra and GT350 and GT500 models, but a thriving parts business put money in everyone's pocket (except the customers). While Mustang owners might not be able to afford a Shelby vehicle, most of them could afford a set of aluminum valve covers, wheels, and an air cleaner. These dress-up parts were big business, and it was a rare car magazine in the 1960s that didn't have a number of ads touting the Shelby name on anything remotely automotive.

Business grew to the point where Shelby needed more production space, and he was able to move into two hangers on Imperial Highway at Los Angeles International Airport leased from North American Aviation. These facilities would serve Shelby until Ford Motor Company decided in 1966 that it needed to exercise more control over the manufacturing process of the GT350 and the soon-to-come GT500. Helping with the decision to relocate was a move by the management at LAX, who owned the land the hangers sat on. They decided that the hangers should be used for aviation-based business, so Shelby had to look for new lodgings. The manufacturing of the cars was transferred to Ionia, Michigan, where they would be built until production stopped in 1970.

Fitted with a 427-cubic-inch, side-oiler V-8, the Super Snake was used as a Goodyear tire test vehicle, covering 500 miles on street tires at an average speed of 142 miles per hour. During the test, the car would exceed 170 miles per hour.

In 1966, Shelby inked a deal with the Hertz Rental Car company, eventually supplying 1,000 GT350Hs to Hertz rental fleets that catered to Walter Mittys. Some of the early Hertz cars were equipped with four-speed manual transmissions, but soon, only automatic-equipped cars were built in an effort to cut down on maintenance costs.

The Mustang grew in size in 1967 as the vehicle was designed to hold a bigger engine. Chevrolet introduced its Mustang fighter for the 1967 model year, and shortly

after its debut, it was available with a big-block engine. Ford reacted to that with a big-block in the Mustang. Pity is, it was only a 390-cubic-inch, yawn-inducing mill. But Shelby was Johnny-on-the-spot, and soon the GT500, equipped with a beefy 428-ci engine, was shredding tires from coast to coast. Working with Goodyear tires, Shelby even installed a fearsome GT40-spec 427-cubic-inch side-oiler V-8 in a GT500, to be used as a tire test vehicle. This car was subjected to a 500-mile tire test, with the car averaging 142 mph, with peak speeds in excess of 170 mph. This was accomplished on street tires. After the test, the car sat on a car lot for a year before it was sold.

Remember the Cobras kicking the Corvette's tail in 1963? It came back to bite Carroll Shelby in his tail in February 1968 when former General Motors executive Semon E. "Bunkie" Knudsen arrived in Dearborn to take the reins at Ford. There was no love lost between Shelby and Knudsen, and as quick as you can say

Shelby had a rich competition history before he started building vehicles with his name on them. He used the lessons learned on the track to construct cars that were equally at home on the street and the starting grid.

When the GT350 debuted, it was a sign that the Shelby Mustangs were starting to step away from pure competition and were becoming more mainstream. While the purists were crying, the car was selling in record numbers.

As the Mustang's proportions grew, so did the Shelby versions. In 1967, that meant a larger interior, but most important, a larger engine compartment. This allowed the installation of a big-block engine, creating the GT500.

"race-winning Cobra," Knudsen initiated the Boss program at Ford, effectively killing the Shelby program.

After he was shown the door at Ford, Shelby followed Lee Iacocca to Chrysler, helping to develop and market a line of front-drive small cars. They didn't do much to fatten the corporate bottom line, but when Robert Lutz took charge of Chrysler, he approached Shelby about a two-seat sports car. The result, the Viper, debuted in 1989 to critical acclaim and continues in production to this day.

When Iacocca retired from Chrysler, Shelby stepped away from the company and started his own firm in Las Vegas. The first car designed and built was the Series 1, a two-seat sports car in the Cobra mold that used an Oldsmobile engine. Sales were not spectacular, and Shelby looked to other projects. In 2002, ties with Ford Motor Company were mended, and Shelby came on board the team that developed the Ford GT. With the success of that vehicle, and the debut of the all-new Mustang in 2005, everything was in place to make history again.

In 2006, Ford SVT worked with Shelby to create the GT500, and since then, a steady stream of enthusiast-pleasing vehicles have been rolling out of

the Shelby plant next to the Las Vegas Motor Speedway. The latest, the GT500 Super Snake, develops 725 horsepower and is only available without a warranty. In order to hold down costs, Shelby and Tasca Ford signed an agreement that has Tasca Ford as an authorized "mod shop," meaning the Rhode Island dealership can modify customers' Mustangs to full Shelby specs. It's not unlike the 1960s, when dealers massaged customers' cars to order. The more things change . . .

Shelby inspired a number of performance dealerships to take a swing at the performance market. Yenko envied Shelby's race successes and the national distribution system that Shelby set up with Ford. Yenko would build a network of Chevrolet dealers to market and sell his vehicles, using his contacts at the highest level of Chevrolet. Tasca Ford worked with Shelby early in the Texan's career as a vehicle maker in distributing the sports cars on the East Coast. Ford Motor Company poured millions of dollars into Shelby's pockets to "help" him win race victories and sell cars. And Shelby used his ambition, smarts, and skill in building one of the most successful performance car programs in history.

Fewer than 90 days passed from the start of construction of the first Cobra Daytona Coupe in October 1963 to its first track test. On March 21, 1964, it earned its first GT-class win and fourth overall at the 12 Hours of Sebring.

Brutally functional, the Cobra Coupe used a Kamm-inspired design at the rear to supply downforce by creating a low-pressure zone. The peerless proportions are evident when seen from this angle.

A 1964 289 Cobra FIA lunges toward the apex of Turn 8A at Laguna Seca Raceway during the 2003 Monterey Historic Automobile Races. Only five FIA Cobras were built. The bulges on the trunk lid are to allow a suitcase to fit—an FIA requirement.

# CHAPTER 12

# EPILOGUE

## *TODAY'S PERFORMANCE*

When the door closed on street-performance vehicles in the early 1970s, the majority of motorists in America didn't bat an eye. Oil embargos, rising insurance costs, and increasingly flaccid powerplants quickly relegated 12-second cars to the history pages. Auto manufacturers worked to design and build cars that were socially responsible, devoid of style and fun. From afar, it looked like Detroit was settling into a period of performance drought, with scant hope on the horizon.

Yet deep in the bowels of the automakers were groups of individuals who grew up on horsepower and smoking tires. They worked in the shadows, toiling under the radar to bring a vestige of verve back into street cars. At the same time, the automotive aftermarket industry was developing components that would let enthusiasts pull a few more ponies from beneath the hood. The salvation of both parties would be built of silicon.

The Boss 302 is one of the iconic names in Mustang history, and the Galpin version lives up to the original's level of performance. Designed as a canyon carver, it handles like a leech on the road, yet the healthy small-block will throw it down a straight line like a rocket.

With its ground-hugging stance, huge wheels and tires, and vivid paint and graphics package, the Galpin Boss 302 is a menacing beast. However, speed bumps and steep driveways must be approached with caution.

If there is a better way to shift gears than to row a T-handled Hurst shifter, I haven't heard of it. A shift light on top of the dashboard next to the driver's side A-pillar helps to cue the driver when the optimal time to shift has arrived.

Under the Shaker hood scoop is a Boss 302 crate engine from Ford Motor Company. Word on the street is that Ford will introduce a Boss Mustang in production form for 2009, but until then, the crew at Galpin Motors is outfitting the beefy engine into a stiffened Mustang body. Designed to put out up to 500 horsepower, the small-block is the next page in Mustang performance.

The huge exhaust pipes aren't there for looks. Admittedly, they do look good, but a performance engine like the Boss 302 crate engine needs to breathe in order to threaten the rear tires.

As the classic performance era wound down, the usage of computers in automobiles was beginning. Not just in the vehicles themselves, but at the engineers' stations. Computers allowed designers and engineers to develop mechanical and electrical systems at a significant savings in time and material. Under the hood, vehicles were using small computers to monitor and adjust engine management components to reduce emissions, improve mileage, and extract more power.

In a replay of the 1960s, a number of individuals were campaigning race cars with quiet factory support. These efforts were ideal test beds for manufacturers to test many of their performance components in a harsh environment. At the same time, the race teams built relationships with the automakers, opening the door to develop more mainstream projects such as street-performance vehicles. As these companies introduced vehicles that leaned heavily toward performance rather than transportation, the public snapped them up as if they were starved for strong acceleration and nimble handling. The strong response from enthusiasts encouraged more firms to build street-legal modern muscle cars.

Today the automotive landscape is filled with plenty of options for the performance junkie. The auto manufacturers themselves are building production cars that would embarrass anything from the 1960s, yet meet emission standards for mainstream cars. No longer is single-digit fuel economy the price paid for performance; today's cars allow enthusiasts to have their power cake and eat it too. While some lament the "Good Old Days" when 47-cent Sunoco 280 was on every corner, we are now in a period of unbelievable street performance. Between the factory offerings and the boutique manufacturers, today's performance enthusiasts are smack in the middle of another Golden Age.

## FACTORY FUN

It's hard to believe, but in today's performance climate, the fun doesn't start until you're packing at

Baer brakes, used on NASCAR racers, work well to shed speed quickly. Progressive, firm, but not grabby, they give superb feel while slowing the Boss 302 as if it dropped an anchor.

least 300 horsepower. While the number isn't as large as in the 1960s, today's power is rated differently, with an engine full of accessories and through the driveline. For instance, Ford had kept the Mustang alive during the Dark Ages of Performance, when a healthy kid on a 10-speed could blow the original Pony Car into the weeds. Fast-forward to today, and the Mustang GT delivers 300 honest, reliable horses on regular pump gas. Buyers wanting yet more power (and don't we all want more power?) are able to walk into any Ford dealership and drive out with a 500-horsepower GT500. This is a 12-second car that will roll through the lights doing 121 mph on street tires, all day long.

Larry Shinoda designed the graphics package on the original Boss 302 Mustangs, and if it ain't broke, don't fix it. Distinctive and instantly identifiable, the "classic" graphics design work wonderfully on the current-generation Mustang.

This Galpin Boss 302 sported a functional Shaker hood scoop, mounted above a Holley four-barrel carburetor. Curling your toe spins the engine up, causing the scoop to quiver and buck.

Of the Big Three automakers, Chrysler was lost in the wilderness the longest, as it put all of its eggs in the front-wheel-drive basket for many years. The merger with Daimler-Benz helped Chrysler to return to its performance past with products such as the Charger, Magnum, and the Challenger. With a 425-horsepower Hemi under the hood, tire smoke was a mandatory option. And you can't forget the scary-fast Viper, now coming at you with an 8.4-liter V-10 that makes 600 horsepower, so that you can get into trouble that much quicker.

General Motors. In the past, nameplates like Camaro, Chevelle, 4-4-2, and Gran Sport were the sound of glory. No company invested more in performance than GM during the 1960s, but when the performance pendulum swung away from power, no

company distanced themselves further from fast cars than General Motors. Granted, the Camaro, Firebird, and Corvette were still available, but they were mere whispers of their former selves. A succession of questionable regimes had the corporation drifting, sometimes making sounds like it wanted to get back into the enthusiast market, other times shunning performance like the plague. Axing the Camaro and Firebird did little to strengthen the ties between company and enthusiasts, but today the Camaro has returned, while the Corvette is boasting up to 600 tire-melting ponies. Pontiac has introduced the imaginatively named G8, a worthy successor to the GTO of old. The sheer size of General Motors has worked against itself at times, especially when performance enters the picture. But the future at GM looks encouraging for enthusiasts.

John Lingenfelter built some of the fastest cars in the world, and the Corvette was one of his favorite platforms. The C5 500TT used twin turbochargers to crank out 500 horsepower and speeds north of 190 miles per hour.

## EXTRACURRICULAR ACTIVITIES

Every year the crazies descend on Las Vegas. Not your regular wackos, waving dollar bills at the roulette wheel and ogling cocktail waitresses. No, these are the hardcore nut jobs attending the annual Specialty Equipment Market Association love-fest. Every square foot of Sin City's convention floor space is filled with every conceivable aftermarket part, car, and gizmo, and a lot you can't conceive of. Auto manufacturers use SEMA as a test market for new products, while boutique vehicle-makers show-case their latest and greatest. And the enthusiasts eat it up like candy. Builders such as Saleen, Callaway, Roush, and Shelby often unveil ever

stronger offerings. In an industry that was facing extinction 30 years ago, there are more performance choices than ever before.

Reeves Callaway got his start hopping up his car in college, raced in Formula Vee and collected the 1973 National Championship, and became fluent in transforming Corvettes into very fast sculpture. In the mid-1980s he worked with Chevrolet to create the B2K option, a twin-turbo setup that was street-legal. Since then, he's built a 255-mph Corvette Sledgehammer, modified Camaros, raced at Le Mans, and created a long line of street-legal mon-sters that utilize current Corvettes as a base vehicle and then add enhancements that result in a brutally

Incredibly fast, the Saleen S7 Twin Turbo can be driven on the street without great effort. Functional ground effects suck the car to the road as the speed increases. You get used to being stared at.

With 750 horsepower, the S7's twin turbo engine will propel the street car to almost 250 miles per hour. A clear engine cover lets passersby gawk at the potent powerplant.

For a supercar, the S7's interior is surprisingly comfortable. Designed to compete in endurance racing, the interior needs to cosset the driver during long stints behind the wheel to keep concentration at a peak.

Near-surgical levels of cleanliness are maintained in the build area at Saleen for the S7. Each car is constructed by a small dedicated team that signs the vehicle at the end of the assembly process.

quick vehicle that is livable as a daily driver. For a score of years, he has worked with General Motors to make buying one of his cars as painless as possible. Once a new Corvette rolls off the assembly line in Bowling Green, Kentucky, it's shipped directly to a Callaway modification center, where the work is done. The finished product is transported to the original selling dealer, where the customer picks it up. This close Callaway/dealer relationship is key to producing a performance car that can be lived with.

Another performance-car builder has racing roots, and today, Saleen continues to build vehicles with a decidedly racing bent. Steve Saleen introduced his first street car in 1984, based on the Ford Mustang, and over the years has built ever-stronger cars. Saleen even manufacturers a two-seat automobile, the S7, which in racing trim has competed in some of the finest endurance races around the world. Today, Saleen offers a wide range of Mustang-sourced street machines with up to 550 horsepower, and even a performance truck. Using a

nationwide distribution system of specially trained Ford dealers, customers can tailor their Saleen to fit their specific needs, and then finance it through the standard dealer process. It's almost pain-free performance. Almost.

Jack Roush got his feet wet in 1976 when he opened his Performance Engineering firm, and today there aren't many motorsports areas that Roush doesn't have a presence in. Much to his competition's chagrin, he's usually winning everything in sight. He has enjoyed a long relationship with Ford Motor Company, and that relationship is evident with the line of Roush Mustangs. Performance junkies can satisfy their power cravings with up to 435 horsepower. A wide range of option packages means an enthusiast can buy just as much power as he or she needs. Roush even sells a version designed to hammer down the quarter-mile, yet it can be driven to work every day.

Former drag-racing champion John Lingenfelter used General Motors vehicles as the starting point for his performance enhancements, including

Part of the Saleen treatment is to lower the vehicle using select performance components and the fitment of wheels and tires larger than the stock Ford units. The result is a Mustang that corners like it's on rails.

With decades of experience racing Mustangs, Saleen is able to deliver reliable horsepower for the street. The S281 comes in various strengths, from a "mere" 335 horsepower up to a license-threatening 550.

In 1990, regular enthusiasts could walk into select Chevrolet dealers and order an RPO B2K, which is GM-speak for Callaway Twin Turbo option. In addition to the price of a regular Corvette, the buyer would write a supplementary check for $26,895.

With 650 horsepower on tap and a starting price of $150,000, Callaway C16 buyers can be confident that they'll have the only one on their block. Building on the famed C6 Corvette platform, Callaway built a race car disguised as a street car.

Body designer Paul Deutschaman crafted a slippery, aggressive shape built of carbon fiber, Kevlar, and fiberglass. The C12 could cover the quarter mile in just 12.8 seconds at 116 miles per hour.

The Callaway Camaro C8 boasted 404 horsepower and 412 lb-ft of torque beneath the long hood. Debuting in 1994, the C8 was fast (172 miles per hour), swoopy, and rare.

Corvettes, a GMC Sonoma, Chevy Cavalier, and Pontiac Trans Am. His engineering prowess led Reeves Callaway to contract Lingenfelter to design and build the 900-horsepower engine used in Callaway's Sledgehammer. In 2001, Lingenfelter sold a street-legal Corvette with 725 horses, enough to merge onto highway traffic. Unfortunately, Lingenfelter was killed in 2003 following an accident while drag racing at the quarter-mile at Pomona, California, but his company continues to develop and sell bespoke performance.

In a déjà vu moment, Baldwin-Motion has returned to 1969, in a sense. Using modern technology, Motion founder Joel Rosen is again offering 1969

Built to stretch its legs on long ribbons of road, the Callaway C12 had a top speed of 188 miles per hour, and its road-holding ability had to be experienced to be believed. Callaway has competed at Le Mans many times, and that experience is reflected in the street cars.

Built to evoke the original Cobra, the Series 1 was a pure two-seat sports car built on a bespoke aluminum chassis and powered by a 4.0-liter Oldsmobile engine. All of the ducts, wings, and scoops were functional, as the Series 1 could reach 170 miles per hour.

With a heavy right foot, and complete disregard for the rear tires, a Series 1 shows what a supercharged V-8 can do. The 2,660-pound car needed just 4.4 seconds to reach 62 miles per hour.

Built at Shelby's Las Vegas, Nevada, facility, the Series 1 production ran from 1998 to 2005.

Camaros for sale. With up to 600 horsepower available in the Phase III package, each car is custom-built for its buyer and can be had in coupe or convertible form. Baldwin-Motion cars were never cheap in the old days, and some things never change. Prices start at $189,000 for the Phase III version. Rosen unveiled

the car at the 2006 SEMA show, and like the original cars, it's the proverbial bigger stick. Some things never go out of style.

Mopar fans don't have to feel ignored in these current times, as Mr. Norm is up to his old tricks. Starting with a 1968 Dodge Dart, a customer can write a check for up to 720 Hemi horsepower. He's building 40 of these earthmovers, and with an option list as long as your arm, the cost of admission is not cheap. But it takes long green to melt tires, and Mr. Norm has always been a tire salesman's best friend.

Last, but by no means least, is Carroll Shelby's latest slate of Mustang-based muscle machines. Long a Ford modifier, he and Ford Motor Company went their separate ways in the 1970s after collaborating on an

When the last generation of the Camaro was introduced, few thought that it would be possible to buy a street-legal, 600-horsepower example. It turned out to be entirely possible. All it took was money, a lot of money.

This number carries substantial historical significance in Camaro circles, and the crew at GMMG tapped into that past with the limited release of the all-aluminum ZL-1 427-cubic-inch V-8.

impressive line of GT350s and GT500s. In the new millennium, Ford and Shelby rejoined, and the results have been an answer to muscle-car enthusiasts' prayers. From a 315-horsepower Shelby GT to a warranty-be-damned 725-horse GT500KR, Shelby and Ford have created a line of performance cars that not only carry on but improve upon the glory days of the 1960s.

The complexities of today's automobiles deter virtually every dealer from duplicating what performance dealers in the 1960s were able to create. One dealership in Southern California, Galpin Ford, has created a large following with its boutique performance shop. Today,

high performance is often as close as a laptop computer, yet Galpin, America's largest Ford dealer, has been able to offer unique street vehicles that are the contemporary version of the "classic" performance dealerships. Using economy of scale, Galpin has resources denied to most modern dealers. This allows them to put specialized performance products on the street.

Gone are the days when grease under the nails and long nights in a closed service department resulted in a fierce car. But for a brief period in America, having the biggest stick on the block just took an open checkbook.

With each GMMG Camaro, essentially a bespoke vehicle, the choice of color was up to the original owner. This shade, Marina Blue, was a popular color on performance Chevrolets in the 1960s.

**Above:** Looking like an arrow on wheels, a Berger Camaro had the beans, 375 of them, to back up the aggressive looks. Like all the best performance cars, they are rare vehicles.

**Left:** This was a view that many would see when running against a late-model Berger Camaro. Even today, Berger is looking to "enhance" the latest-generation Camaro.

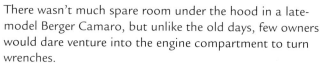

There wasn't much spare room under the hood in a late-model Berger Camaro, but unlike the old days, few owners would dare venture into the engine compartment to turn wrenches.

Berger didn't believe in festooning its cars with splashy graphics, instead preferring the vehicle's performance to do the talking. Starting with a Camaro SS meant that a slew of factory performance parts were already installed.

The lineage is unmistakable, as the 1967 Shelby GT500 Super Snake and the 2008 version share a lonely stretch of road. Neither car is really hitting its stride until the speedometer starts reading in the triple digits.

With a big supercharger on top and beefy mechanicals below, the Super Snake can be outfitted to generate 725 horsepower if the owner is willing to live without a warranty.

Until the 2008 Super Snake debuted, the one-and-only 1967 Shelby GT500 Super Snake was the only Shelby vehicle with three stripes. The new car is available in two flavors, 650 horsepower and 725 ponies.

Sitting on special 18-inch alloy wheels, the Roush 427R is a menacing-looking vehicle, especially in black. With 427 horsepower at hand, care must be taken to keep it pointed in the right direction.

Somewhere under all of the plastic is a very healthy 4.6-liter engine. Topped with a supercharger, the Roush engineers were able to withdraw 427 horsepower, quite a feat using pump gasoline.

As its name implies, the intercooled, supercharged 4.6-liter V-8 under the hood of the Roush 427R produces that many horsepower. The distinctive stripe is unique to Roush Mustangs.

Jack Roush has been involved in motorsports for years, and he brings a heavy dose of that flavor to the 427R Mustang. From the functional front air dam to the rear wing, this is a serious road machine with an MSRP of $58,245. Such a deal!

# INDEX